D1267136

Great Meals in Minutes was created by
Rebus, Inc.
and published by Time-Life Books.

Rebus, Inc.

Publisher: Rodney Friedman
Editorial Director: Shirley Tomkievicz

Editor: Marya Dalrymple
Art Director: Ronald Gross
Managing Editor: Brenda Goldberg
Senior Editor: Charles Blackwell
Food Editor and Food Stylist: Grace Young
Photographer: Steven Mays
Prop Stylist: Cathryn Schwing
Staff Writer: Alexandra Greeley
Associate Editor: Ann M. Harvey
Assistant Editor: Bonnie J. Slotnick
Assistant Food Stylist: Karen Hatt
Photography Assistant: Glenn Maffei
Recipe Tester: Gina Palombi Barclay
Production Assistant: Lorna Bieber

For information about any Time-Life book,
please write:
Reader Information
Time-Life Books
541 North Fairbanks Court
Chicago, Illinois 60611

Library of Congress Cataloging in Publication Data
Pork & ham menus.
    (Great meals in minutes)
    Includes index.
    1. Cookery (Ham) 2. Cookery (Pork)
    3. Cooks—United States—Biography.
I. Time-Life Books. II. Title:
Pork and ham menus. III. Series.
TX749.P66 1985   641.59'64   84-16319
ISBN 0-86706-199-5 (lib. bdg.)
ISBN 0-86706-198-7 (retail ed.)

© 1985 Time-Life Books Inc. All rights reserved.
No part of this book may be reproduced in any
form or by any electronic or mechanical means,
including information storage and retrieval
devices or systems, without prior written
permission from the publisher, except that brief
passages may be quoted for reviews.
First printing. Printed in U.S.A.
Published simultaneously in Canada.
School and library distribution by Silver Burdett
Company, Morristown, New Jersey.

TIME-LIFE is a trademark of Time Incorporated
U.S.A.

Time-Life Books Inc.
is a wholly owned subsidiary of
Time Incorporated

Founder: Henry R. Luce 1898–1967

Editor-in-Chief: Henry Anatole Grunwald
President: J. Richard Munro
Chairman of the Board: Ralph P. Davidson
Corporate Editor: Jason McManus
Group Vice President, Books: Reginald K.
Brack Jr.

Time-Life Books Inc.

Editor: George Constable
Executive Editor: George Daniels
Director of Design: Louis Klein
Board of Editors: Roberta Conlan,
Ellen Phillips, Gerry Schremp, Gerald
Simons, Rosalind Stubenberg, Kit van
Tulleken, Henry Woodhead
Editorial General Manager: Neal Goff
Director of Research: Phyllis K. Wise
Director of Photography: John Conrad Weiser

President: Reginald K. Brack Jr.
Senior Vice President: William Henry
Vice Presidents: George Artandi, Stephen L.
Bair, Robert A. Ellis, Juanita T. James,
Christopher T. Linen, James L. Mercer,
Joanne A. Pello, Paul R. Stewart

Editorial Operations
Design: Ellen Robling (assistant director)
Copy Room: Diane Ullius
Production: Ann B. Landry (director), Celia
Beattie
Quality Control: James J. Cox (director), Sally
Collins
Library: Louise D. Forstall

SERIES CONSULTANT
Margaret E. Happel is the author of *Ladies
Home Journal Adventures in Cooking*,
*Ladies Home Journal Handbook of Holiday
Cuisine*, and other best-selling cookbooks, as
well as the translator and adapter of Rebecca
Hsu Hiu Min's *Delights of Chinese Cooking*.
A food consultant based in New York City,
she has been director of the food department
of *Good Housekeeping* and editor of
American Home magazine.

WINE CONSULTANT
Tom Maresca combines a full-time career
teaching English literature with writing
about and consuming fine wines. He is now
at work on *The Wine Case Book*, which
explains the techniques of wine tasting.

Cover: Holly Garrison's American *choucroute
garnie*, pan-roasted yams, and beet and
lettuce salad with mustard vinaigrette,
pages 30–32.

Great Meals
IN MINUTES

PORK & HAM
MENUS

TIME-LIFE BOOKS, ALEXANDRIA, VIRGINIA

Contents

Meet the Cooks

LUCY WING
A native of Arizona, Lucy Wing began her food career as a home economist in the Best Foods Division of CPC International Inc. After several editorial jobs at national magazines, she became food and equipment editor for *American Home* magazine. She is contributing food editor for *McCall's* and has written articles for *Country Living*, *SELF*, *Cuisine*, and *Family Circle*.

HOLLY GARRISON
Born in Reading, Pennsylvania, Holly Garrison has been interested in cooking and fine food for most of her life. Trained as a journalist, she also attended cooking classes in the United States and in Europe. She is the food editor of *Parents* magazine.

DAVID KIMMEL AND STEVEN PETUSEVSKY
David Kimmel and his colleague Steven Petusevsky are both graduates of the Culinary Institute of America. David Kimmel has taught restaurant design at the Institute and is a member of its board of trustees. Steven Petusevsky has been employed by several hotels, among them the Woodstock Inn and the Frankfurt Inter-Continental. Since 1982 they have worked together at Caraway Associates, a New York-based food-consulting company.

W. PETER PRESTCOTT
W. Peter Prestcott has owned and managed two restaurants as well as a New York-based catering firm and has worked as executive chef for a restaurant chain in California. He developed the test kitchen for *Food & Wine* and writes a regular feature on entertaining for that magazine.

DENNIS GILBERT

After graduate school, Dennis Gilbert decided to combine two careers: cooking and writing. He apprenticed with a chef in Maine and trained in restaurants specializing in classical and regional French cooking. He is now *chef de cuisine* at the Vinyard Restaurant in Portland, Maine, and teaches English at the University of Southern Maine. His short stories have appeared in numerous publications.

MERYLE EVANS

Meryle Evans has worked as a consultant for the New-York Historical Society and has been an editor of several books, including *The American Heritage Cookbook* and *American Manners and Morals*. She regularly contributes food articles to the *New York Times* and to *Food & Wine* magazine, and owns a large collection of antique American cookware.

LEE HAIKEN

Lee Haiken, who describes herself as a self-taught cook, has worked extensively in the food field. She founded the North Shore Cooking School and North Shore Catering on Long Island, and has given cooking demonstrations and served as a judge in many national cooking contests. For the past nine years, she has been food editor of *Weight Watchers*® magazine.

LEON, STANLEY, AND EVAN LOBEL

For five generations, members of the Lobel family have worked in the retail meat business. Today brothers Leon and Stanley Lobel and Leon's son Evan run the family butcher shop on Madison Avenue in New York City. The Lobels are the co-authors of four books, including *All About Meat*, and together they write a syndicated weekly newspaper column. Both Leon and Stanley have taught classes, and Evan has taught meat preparation and butchering at several cooking schools.

ALICE ROSS

Alice Ross teaches food history and ethnic cuisines at Queens College in New York, and regularly writes food articles for *Newsday*, the Long Island daily newspaper. A Ph.D. candidate in food history at the State University of New York at Stony Brook, she also conducts workshops in hearth cookery for museums and private groups.

Pork & Ham Menus in Minutes

GREAT MEALS FOR FOUR IN AN HOUR OR LESS

Bacon. Sausage. Roast suckling pig. Spareribs. Chitterlings. Pickled pig's feet. Pork chops. Ham. From snout to tail, virtually every part of the pig is edible. No wonder the noted French gourmand Grimod de la Reynière described this hearty animal as a "veritable walking repast." Today—as it has been for thousands of years—pork is the most popular meat in the world.

Rich in vitamins, particularly thiamine, and in minerals such as iron and zinc, pork also contains all eight essential amino acids, which makes it an excellent source of protein. According to USDA statistics, today's pig is 50 percent leaner than the pig of 1950, and, with just 198 calories in a three-ounce serving of fresh pork, dieters need no longer consider this a forbidden food. In fact, that same three ounces of pork has only a modest amount of cholesterol—less than an equivalent serving of veal, dark-meat turkey, or lamb.

Although Stone Age man undoubtedly hunted and ate wild boar, it was probably the Chinese who first domesticated pigs around 5000 B.C. (the Chinese ideogram for "home" is a pig beneath a roof). By 1500 B.C. pigs were being raised in Europe, and for centuries thereafter pork was practically the only meat the peasantry ever tasted.

Pigs were brought to Cuba by Christopher Columbus in 1493 and to America by Hernando de Soto, who landed at what is now Tampa Bay in 1539 with 13 hogs on board. Three years later, his fledgling herd had grown to more than 700 head, the beginning of America's pork supply. Until the mid-twentieth century, pork was America's favorite meat, particularly in the South, and "eating high on the hog" meant bountiful dining. Today beef outranks pork in popularity in this country, but the United States still produces more pigs than any other country except China, and Americans consume 15 billion pounds of pork annually.

More prolific than any other type of livestock, a sow can produce a litter of eight piglets every five months. Farmers carefully monitor the diet of pigs slated for market (feeding their animals balanced rations of corn and other grains, protein supplements, vitamins, and minerals) to improve their rate of growth and the flavor of the meat. A properly fed pig gains twice as much weight per pound of feed as any other animal raised for food and produces 67 percent retail meat at slaughter, compared with about 46 percent for cattle. About a third of each animal's meat is sold as fresh cuts, and the rest is turned into processed pork products such as ham, sausage, and bacon.

Economical and widely available, pork plays an important role in most of the world's cuisines. On the following pages, nine of America's most talented cooks present 27 complete menus, with recipes from the United States, Scandinavia, France, Mexico, Germany, Indonesia, Thailand, China, Greece, and Italy, all featuring fresh or processed pork or ham. Every recipe uses fresh produce and good cuts of meat. Additional ingredients (vinegars, spices, herbs, and so on) are all high quality yet widely available in supermarkets or occasionally in specialty food shops. Each of the menus serves four people. All recipes have been tested meticulously to ensure that even a relatively inexperienced cook can complete a menu within an hour. The cooks and the test kitchen staff have planned the meals for appearance as well as taste, as the accompanying photographs show: The vegetables are brilliant and fresh, the visual combinations appetizing. The table settings feature bright colors, simple flower arrangements, and attractive but not necessarily expensive serving dishes.

For each menu, the Editors, with advice from the cooks, suggest wines and other beverages. And there are suggestions for the use of leftovers and for complementary desserts. On each menu page, too, you will find a range of other tips, from an easy method for stuffing pork rolls to advice for selecting the freshest produce.

BEFORE YOU START

Great Meals in Minutes is designed for efficiency and ease. This book will work best for you if you follow these suggestions:

1. Read the guidelines (pages 8 to 11) for selecting fresh pork, ham, sausage, and bacon.

2. Refresh your memory with the few simple cooking techniques on the following pages. They will quickly become second nature and will help you to produce professional-quality meals in minutes.

3. Read the menus before you shop. Each lists the ingredients you will need, in the order that you would expect

Fresh pork, ham, and sausages, as well as appropriate fruits, vegetables and herbs, await preparation. Clockwise, from top left: a whole Smithfield ham; a pork loin roast with parsley and rosemary; a red cabbage; a center-cut ham steak; pork chops with prunes and a plum; and a string of Italian link sausages with sage leaves.

to shop for them. You will already have many items.

4. Check the equipment list on page 16. Good, sharp knives and pots and pans of the right shape and material are essential for making great meals in minutes. This may be the time to buy a few things. The right equipment can turn cooking from a necessity into a creative experience.

5. Set out everything you need before you start to cook: The lists at the beginning of each menu tell just what is required. To save effort, always keep your ingredients in the same place so you can reach for them instinctively.

6. Follow the start-to-finish steps for each menu. That way, you can have the entire meal ready in an hour.

SELECTING, STORING, AND COOKING FRESH PORK

Pork carcasses are first split and then divided into primal cuts: Boston shoulder, picnic shoulder, side or belly, leg, and loin. These are subdivided into the various retail cuts, such as ribs, roasts, and chops. Nearly all pork cuts are consistently tender because pigs are slaughtered before they are a year old. Consequently, USDA grades such as PRIME, CHOICE, and GOOD, which are used to indicate beef tenderness, are not applied to cuts of pork sold at retail, nor does fresh pork need to undergo the aging required to tenderize beef.

Although pork is tender throughout, it still helps to know which part of the carcass your cut is from so you know how to cook it. The forequarters of the pig have small muscles with many connective tissues; thus meat from this part (such as the boneless shoulder) tends to be more fibrous than meat from other parts of the pig and should be cooked by a moist-heat method such as braising. Freshly ground pork is also made from this part. The hindquarters of the pig contain large muscles with few connective tissues, so the meat here (such as boneless leg) is more tender and suitable for roasting or frying. The less-developed back muscles, where the loin is located, produce the tenderest cuts, which can be cooked by any method. (See the box on page 9 for more specific information about the fresh pork used in this book.)

When purchasing fresh pork, look for firmly textured flesh with a moderate amount of marbling (or interior fat running through the meat) and a moderate layer of white exterior fat. Fresh pork ranges in color from grayish-pink to deep rose. Some cuts, particularly the loin, may have a slightly two-toned appearance (pearly white tinged with pink), which is also acceptable. Shoulder cuts and legs are generally darker, with a coarser texture. Any visible bones should be red and spongy at the ends, not white and hard. Avoid pork that looks dry, feels soft to the touch, or that has dark-pink meat and yellowed fat. Prepackaged ground pork, a relatively new product in many areas, is at least 70 percent lean and contains no seasonings. Fresh pork has no odor.

Read the package label carefully; it will indicate the type of cut, weight, price per pound, total price, and sometimes a date after which the pork should not be sold. Do not buy pork after this date.

Like all fresh meat, fresh pork must be stored in the meat compartment or in the coldest part of the refrigerator to maintain its quality. If you buy prepackaged fresh pork from the supermarket, store the meat in its original wrapping. If you buy fresh pork from a butcher, unwrap the meat from the butcher's paper and loosely rewrap it in plastic or foil. Ground fresh pork will keep for one to two days, and fresh pork cuts will remain fresh for three to four days. Store cooked fresh pork well wrapped for no longer than three or four days.

You can freeze fresh pork wrapped tightly in a moisture-proof material, such as specially coated freezer paper, foil, or heavy-duty transparent wrap. Seal the package with freezer tape and label it with the date and type of cut. Frozen pork cuts will keep for up to six months; freshly ground pork up to three months. Let pork thaw in the refrigerator, or unwrap it and thaw it during cooking in a regular or microwave oven. Never defrost pork at room temperature, and be sure to cook thawed pork immediately. Never refreeze thawed pork.

Pork is safe to eat when it has been cooked to an internal temperature of 140 degrees. However, cooking it to a higher temperature—170 degrees is often recommended—will result in juicier, more flavorful meat. Be careful not to overcook the meat: It should still be slightly pink inside. An instant-reading meat thermometer is an essential tool for cooking perfect pork.

BUYING, STORING, AND COOKING HAM, SAUSAGE, AND BACON

Most pork is cured after slaughter. In the days before refrigeration, curing was essentially the application of salt to remove moisture and preserve the meat. It resulted in a dry, hard product that would last for at least a year without spoiling. Today color, flavor, and yield rather than preservation are the object of curing, and modern quick-curing methods draw minimal moisture from the meat. Thus processed pork products are more perishable and must be treated as if they were fresh.

Ham

From the Old English word, *hamm*, which meant thigh, ham today refers to the hind leg of a pig. Ham can be purchased fresh (called fresh leg of pork), but the word generally means a cured or cured and smoked product.

There are hundreds of different types of ham from around the world, their flavors reflecting the differences in the pigs' breeding and diet, the ingredients used in curing, and the wood used if the meat is smoked. Most hams are cured by one of two basic methods: wet cure and dry cure. Although some wet-cured hams are simply immersed in a solution of salt, sugar, and preservatives to enhance their color and flavor and to prevent the growth of organisms, the more common wet-cure method in the United States is injection (or quick) curing. In this method, the meat is deeply injected with a curing solution and allowed to age for 24 hours to a week. Injection-cured hams are rarely smoked.

The second method, dry curing, produces the famous

Pork and Pork Products in This Volume

FRESH PORK

Ground pork: Usually from the front of the pig or from meat trimmings. To grind fresh pork at home, buy a boneless pork shoulder or purchase lean trimmings. See Holly Garrison's Menu 1 (page 28).

Boneless shoulder: From the front leg of the pig. Relatively tough and fatty. Usually tied with string or encased in plastic netting. See Peter Prestcott's Menu 1 (page 48).

Country-style ribs: Cut from the front or blade end of the loin. Leaner and more tender than spareribs, with which they are frequently confused. See Dennis Gilbert's Menu 1 (page 58).

Blade Boston roast, boneless: Cut from the upper front leg of the pig. Can be relatively tough. The meat from this roast is often cubed for kebabs. May also be sold as boneless Boston butt roast. See Lee Haiken's Menu 3 (page 81).

Pork loin top loin roast, boneless: Cut from the loin. The leanest part of the pig. Also known as boneless pork loin roast. See Lucy Wing's Menu 1 (page 20).

Center loin roast, boneless: Cut from the center loin. May also be sold as center cut pork loin, boneless. See Dennis Gilbert's Menu 2 (page 60).

Smoked pork center loin roast: Cut from the center loin, cured and smoked for extra flavor. See Holly Garrison's Menu 2 (page 30).

Eye of loin: Cut from the loin. Largest muscle running through loin. Very tender. Also sold as loin eye. See Peter Prestcott's Menu 2 (page 50).

Loin chops: Cut from the center loin. Contain loin muscles and backbone. Very tender. See Meryle Evans's Menu 1 (page 68).

Rib chops: Cut from the shoulder end of the loin. Contain loin eye muscle and backbone. Rib bone may be present, depending on thickness of chop. See Leon, Stanley, and Evan Lobel's Menu 1 (page 86).

Tenderloin: Cut from the rear of the loin. The most tender cut of pork. May be sliced into medallions and scallops. See David Kimmel and Steven Petusevsky's Menu 1 (page 38).

HAM

Ready-to-eat or fully cooked ham: A cured ham; precooked to an internal temperature of 140 degrees. May be reheated if desired. Readily available at most supermarkets. See Meryle Evans's Menu 2 (page 70).

Country ham: Very salty, dry-cured ham with wine-red flesh; often aged up to one year. Usually requires soaking and simmering to draw out salt. May be named for the state of origin, for example, Georgia or Virginia ham. Available by special order from butchers or at specialty food shops or through the mail (see page 103).

Smithfield ham: The most renowned country ham. To be authentic, this ham must be labeled as processed in Smithfield, Virginia. Cured by a complex method, it has a dark Burgundy color, firm, dry, chewy texture, and an assertive flavor. Quite salty. To order, contact a mail-order supplier (see page 103), or order through a butcher. See Holly Garrison's Menu 3 (page 33).

Prosciutto: An unsmoked, raw, dry-cured Italian-style ham with a dark-pink color and mild flavor. Available at Italian groceries or at the delicatessen counter of well-stocked supermarkets. Because of import restrictions on raw meat, all prosciutto sold in the United States is produced here; however, it closely resembles the Italian product. Needs no further cooking as the intensity of the cure makes it safe to eat. See Alice Ross's Menu 2 (page 98).

Serrano: A raw Spanish-style ham made from lean pork and cured by soaking in wine for several months, after which it is coated with an olive oil and paprika paste and dried. Like prosciutto, this ham cannot be imported and is currently being produced in the United States. It can be found at specialty food shops. See Alice Ross's Menu 2 (page 98).

Westphalian ham: A German-style dry-cured ham with a dark-brown color and rich, smoky taste. Like prosciutto, it needs no further cooking. Available at specialty food shops. See Dennis Gilbert's Menu 2 (page 60).

SAUSAGE

Chorizo: Highly seasoned, coarsely ground Spanish and Mexican fresh sausage; usually removed from casing and crumbled for cooking. Both made from pork, but Mexican type is spicier. Sold in bulk or links at butcher shops, gourmet shops, and some supermarkets. See Alice Ross's Menu 2 (page 98).

Linguiça: Garlicky smoked dry sausage originating in Portugal; also popular in Brazil. The Spanish version is called *longaniza* and may be substituted. See Alice Ross's Menu 2 (page 98).

Italian link sausage: Fresh pork sausage sold as links or in bulk; both sweet and hot varieties are flavored with garlic and fennel. May be cooked in casings or removed from casings and crumbled. Available at most supermarkets and Italian groceries. See Meryle Evans's Menu 3 (page 72).

Kielbasa: Polish specialty; comes fresh or cooked smoked. Highly seasoned with garlic and spices. Found at most supermarkets in large rings or long links. See Holly Garrison's Menu 2 (page 30).

Mild fresh sausage: Ground fresh pork, lightly seasoned with salt, pepper, sugar, and spices. Commonly available in rolls, patties, and links; should be handled like any fresh meat and never tasted before cooking. See Holly Garrison's Menu 1 (page 28).

Smithfield and other country hams as well as renowned European hams such as prosciutto. Pigs intended for dry-cured ham are fed special diets (which include hickory nuts, acorns, or chestnuts) to impart special flavoring to the meat. After slaughter, the meat is rubbed with salt, preservatives, sugar, and seasonings, and kept in a cool place until the seasonings penetrate the meat and the salt extracts much of the moisture. The hams are sometimes smoked and then aged for up to two years. Only a small percentage of hams are cured this way today, but they are

SAFETY NOTES

Cooking at high temperatures will be less dangerous if you follow a few simple tips:

▶ Water added to hot fat will always cause spattering. If possible, pat foods dry with a cloth or paper towel before you add them to the hot oil.

▶ Place food gently into any pan containing hot fat, or the fat will spatter.

▶ If you are boiling or steaming some foods while sautéing others, place the pots on the stove top far enough apart so that the water is unlikely to splash into the hot fat.

▶ Turn pot handles inward, so that you do not accidentally knock over a pot containing hot foods or liquids.

▶ Remember that alcohol—wine, brandy, or spirits—may occasionally catch fire when you add it to a very hot pan. If this happens, step back for your own protection and quickly cover the pan with a lid. The fire will instantly subside, and the food will not be spoiled.

▶ Keep pot holders and mitts close enough to be handy while cooking, but *never* hang them over the burners or lay them on the stove top.

---

sought after by connoisseurs for their firm texture and intense flavor.

Many people consider Smithfield ham to be the finest ham produced in America. Authentic Smithfields are produced in an area defined by a Virginia law of 1926, which states that they must be "cut from carcasses of peanut-fed hogs raised in the peanut belt of the State of Virginia or the State of North Carolina and...cured, treated, smoked and processed in the Town of Smithfield, in the State of Virginia." Smithfield ham is characterized by its "long cut" (which includes most of the hind leg) as well as its heavy coating of black pepper. It is smoked over hickory wood and then aged. Smithfield hams are available by mail from the packers and occasionally from specialty food shops (see page 103 for mail-order suppliers).

Ham is sold in many different forms at supermarkets or butcher shops. It may be whole (bone-in) or have some or all of the bones removed (semi-boneless or boneless). Generally the bone-in hams are most flavorful. Ham typically has a deep-pink color, finely textured meat, and firm white

fat. If the ham is sealed in plastic or canned, check for an expiration date. The best insurance for quality ham is to buy it from a reliable butcher.

Store hams in the refrigerator in their original wrapping or container. Canned hams will keep for several months, other wet-cured hams for a week, and whole dry-cured hams indefinitely. Wrap any leftovers in plastic (the salt used in curing will corrode foil) and keep them in the refrigerator for no longer than three or four days. You can freeze ham tightly sealed in freezer paper or heavy-duty plastic wrap for up to a month. If kept frozen longer, the fat will turn rancid.

Wet-cured hams, whether canned, vacuum packed in plastic, or sold by the pound or slice, will be labeled READY TO EAT, FULLY COOKED, or COOK BEFORE EATING. If the ham is not identified in this way, ask the butcher which type it is. Ready-to-eat and fully cooked hams are safe to eat without further cooking; however, their palatability is greatly enhanced by heating, even if they are to be served cold later. Bake these hams in a moderate oven (325 degrees) to an internal temperature of 140 degrees. Heat cook-before-eating hams to about 170 degrees, as you would fresh pork. American country hams, because they have been smoked at high heat, do not need further cooking, but the directions accompanying them usually call for soaking and cooking the hams for better flavor. (See the box on page 11 for more information on cooking country ham.)

Sausage

Pork sausage originated from the economical salvaging of the trimmings left after butchering pigs, though today it is a product prized by many cuisines. The texture of the grind, the blend of seasonings, and the method of cooking, curing, or smoking give sausages their individual character (see the box on page 9 for information about specific sausages used in this volume). In general, sausage falls into three categories:

Fresh sausage: Made from fresh raw uncured chopped or ground pork (or a combination of meats), this product is sold in bulk, in patties, or enclosed in natural or synthetic casings. Choose fresh sausage as you would any fresh

---

Applesauce

Applesauce, a favorite side dish for pork and other meats, also can be warmed, sweetened, and served with cinnamon and cream for a dessert or breakfast. Plan to double or triple this recipe to make enough applesauce to serve with another meal or two.

Beverly Cox's Tart Applesauce

2 tart cooking apples, peeled, cored, and quartered
1 cup unsweetened apple cider or juice
Zest of 1 lemon
1 teaspoon honey (optional)

1. Combine all ingredients in a small, heavy-gauge saucepan and cook over medium heat 8 to 10 minutes, or until apples are tender.
2. Purée apple mixture in food processor or mash with fork. To serve warm, return to saucepan and reheat over low heat or serve at room temperature.

Serves 4

meat, and treat it as carefully. All fresh pork sausage should be cooked until its center is no longer pink. Though some fresh sausage is smoked (usually at a low temperature), it still requires thorough cooking. Keep fresh sausage tightly wrapped and refrigerated and use it within a week. It will keep in the freezer for up to two months.

Cooked sausage: This type of sausage, made from cured or uncured meat, seasonings, and binders such as nonfat dry milk or flour, has been precooked and sometimes smoked for flavor, or it may have been smoked at temperatures high enough to eliminate the need for cooking. Though ready to eat, the flavor of many fully cooked sausages is enhanced by further cooking. Cooked sausage will keep for up to a week in the refrigerator. Freezing is not recommended, as the sausage will deteriorate quickly.

Dry sausage: Dry sausage originated in the warm countries of southern Europe, where the drying process was necessary to preserve the meat. Some varieties of dry sausage are still called summer sausage because they keep well. Dry sausages are ready to eat, although in this volume they are included in cooked dishes primarily to add flavor. This type of sausage will keep at room temperature for a short time, but for best flavor and wholesomeness, it should be refrigerated and used within three weeks. Do not freeze dry sausage.

Bacon

Bacon is cured (and usually smoked) belly pork, characterized by striations of fat and lean. In the United States, bacon is most often sold presliced in packages marked THIN, REGULAR, or THICK; however, it may also come in slabs that you can cut as needed or have cut to order by a butcher. Bacon should be bright pinkish-red with a fine texture and ivory-colored fat. In good bacon, the fat to lean ratio is about equal.

Unopened vacuum-packed bacon will keep for two to three weeks in the refrigerator; once opened, the bacon will keep for a week. Slab bacon can be stored for up to six weeks, carefully wrapped and refrigerated. Pre-cut and slab bacon, either unopened in the original vacuum-sealed package or well-wrapped, may be frozen for a month, but it will deteriorate markedly if kept longer.

Although bacon is often eaten as a breakfast meat, its flavorful fat is also an excellent frying medium. To prevent excessive shrinkage when cooking bacon, start it in a cold pan and cook it over medium heat. To render the fat for cooking, quickly sauté the bacon in a hot pan, removing the crisped lean when the fat has melted.

GENERAL COOKING TECHNIQUES

Sautéing

Sautéing is a form of quick frying, with no cover on the pan. In French, *sauter* means "to jump," which is what vegetables or small pieces of food do when you shake the sauté pan. The purpose is to brown the food lightly and seal in the juices, sometimes before further cooking. This technique has three critical elements: the right pan, the proper temperature, and dry food.

The sauté pan: A proper sauté pan is 10 to 12 inches in diameter and has 2- to 3-inch straight sides; it allows you to turn the pieces of food and still keep the fat from spattering. It has a heavy bottom that can be moved back and forth easily across a burner.

The best material (and the most expensive) for a sauté pan is tin-lined copper because it is a superior heat conductor. Heavy-gauge cast aluminum works well but will discolor acidic food like tomatoes. Another option is to select a heavy-duty sauté pan made of strong, heat-conducting aluminum alloys. This type of professional cookware is smooth and stick-resistant. Be sure you buy a sauté pan with a handle that is long and comfortable to hold, and with a tight-fitting cover, since many recipes call for covered cooking following the initial sautéing.

Use a sauté pan large enough to hold the pieces of food without crowding, or sauté in two batches. The heat of the fat and the air spaces around and between the pieces facilitate browning. Crowding results in steaming, which releases juices.

Use a wooden spoon or tongs to keep the pieces of food moving in the pan as you shake the pan over the burner. If the food sticks, as it occasionally will, a metal spatula will loosen it best. Turn the food pieces so that all surfaces come into contact with the hot fat. Do not use a fork when sautéing meat; piercing the meat will allow the juices to escape, causing the meat to become tough and dry.

The fat: Half butter and half vegetable oil is perfect for most sautéing: The combination heats to high temperatures without burning, yet imparts a rich butter flavor. For cooking, unsalted butter tastes best and adds no unwanted salt to the recipe.

Cooking a Country Ham

Smithfield and other country hams often make a bad first impression when removed from their cloth bags or wrappers because they have smoke-blackened, crusty, and sometimes moldy exteriors. People have been known to throw away these painstakingly prepared meats because they appear to be spoiled. A few simple steps will make a fine country ham as appealing to the eye as it will be to the palate.

Scrub the whole ham with a stiff brush or a nylon dish scrubber under hot running water. Then soak the ham to remove some of the salt, following the packer's directions; if no directions are included, immerse the ham in cold water in a large pot and soak it for 12 to 24 hours, changing the water twice during this time. After soaking, scrub the ham again, return it to the pot, and add fresh water to cover. Slowly bring the water to a gentle simmer and cook the ham about 20 minutes per pound, or until the protruding bone can be moved easily. Remove from the heat, and when the ham is cool enough to handle, skin it and trim all but about one-quarter inch of the fat. The ham is now ready to eat as is, or to be glazed and baked in a 400- to 450-degree oven for another 20 minutes. See page 103 for where to order a country ham.

If you prefer an all-butter flavor, clarify the butter before you begin. This means removing the milk solids (which scorch easily) from the oils. To clarify butter, heat it in a small heavy-gauge saucepan over medium heat and, using a cooking spoon, skim off the foam as it rises to the top and discard it. Keep skimming until no more foam appears. Pour off the remaining liquid, which is the clarified butter, leaving the milky residue at the bottom of the pan. Clarify butter as you need it, or to save time, make a large quantity and store it in the refrigerator for up to three weeks.

Some sautéing recipes in this book call for olive oil, which imparts a delicious and distinctive flavor of its own and is less sensitive than butter to high heat. Nevertheless, even the finest olive oil has some residue of fruit pulp, which will occasionally scorch. Watch carefully when you sauté in olive oil; discard any scorched oil and start with fresh, if necessary.

To sauté properly, heat the fat until it is hot but not smoking. When you see small bubbles on top of the fat, lower the heat because it is on the verge of smoking. When using butter and oil together, add butter to the hot oil. After the foam from the melting butter subsides, you are ready to sauté. If the temperature of the fat is just right, the food will sizzle when you put it in the pan.

Searing

Searing is somewhat like sautéing, but you need slightly hotter fat. When you sear, you brown the meat without shaking or stirring the pan. Heat the oil until it is very hot, then brown the meat over high heat for a minute or two on each side. A metal spatula is essential, for the meat will tend to stick. Wait until the meat is very brown on one side before you turn it. David Kimmel and Steven Petusevsky sear pork medallions (page 38).

Stir Frying

This is the basic cooking method for Chinese cuisine. This fast-cook technique requires very little oil, and the foods—which you stir continuously—fry quickly over very high heat. Stir frying is ideal for cooking bite-size, shredded, or thinly sliced portions of vegetables, fish, meat, or poultry, alone or in combination. Lucy Wing uses this technique for cooking broccoli (page 25).

Braising

Braising is the simmering of meats or vegetables in a relatively small amount of liquid, usually for a long period of time. Occasionally foods that do not need tenderizing may be braised more quickly to impart flavor. Sometimes the food is browned or parboiled before braising. You may wish to flavor the braising liquid with herbs, spices, and aromatic vegetables, or use wine, stock, or tomato sauce as a medium. Peter Prestcott uses this method to prepare pork tenderloin and fennel (page 51).

Blanching

Blanching, also called parboiling, is an invaluable technique. Immerse whole or cut vegetables for a few moments in boiling water, then refresh them, that is, plunge them into cold water to stop their cooking and set their colors. Blanching softens or tenderizes dense or crisp vegetables, often as a preliminary to further cooking by another method, such as stir frying. Lee Haiken blanches Swiss chard leaves (page 77).

Steaming

Steaming is a fast and nutritious way to cook vegetables and other food. Bring water to a boil in a saucepan. Place the food in a steamer or on a rack over the liquid and cover the pan, periodically checking the water level. Keeping the food above the liquid preserves vitamins and minerals often lost in other methods of cooking. David Kimmel and Steven Petusevsky steam new potatoes (page 39).

Glazing

Glazing vegetables in their cooking liquid, butter, and a little sugar gives them a slight sheen as the butter and sugar reduce to a syrupy consistency. Glazing enhances the flavor and appearance of the vegetables, which then need no additional sauce. Peter Prestcott glazes mushrooms in port wine (page 55).

Broiling and Grilling

These are two relatively fast ways to cook meat, poultry, and fish, giving the food a crisp exterior while leaving the inside juicy. Whether broiling or grilling, brush the food with melted fat, a sauce, or a marinade before you cook. This adds flavor and moisture.

Pork and Health

Like all meats sold in the United States, pork is inspected for wholesomeness. Even so, inspection cannot determine the presence of *trichinae*, microscopic parasites that are the cause of trichinosis in humans. Although in recent years trichinosis has become quite rare, it is still absolutely necessary to observe certain precautions when handling and cooking raw pork and uncooked pork products.

Never taste raw pork, sausage, or bacon when cooking. If you must check ground pork or fresh sausage for seasoning, thoroughly cook a small amount first, taste it, and then season the rest accordingly.

Kitchen utensils—particularly wooden cutting boards and dishes—as well as your hands should be thoroughly washed with hot, soapy water after coming into contact with raw pork. When grinding raw pork or making fresh sausage, sterilize the meat grinder with boiling water.

Fresh pork must be cooked to an internal temperature of at least 140 degrees. For best flavor and tenderness, most recipes recommend a temperature of about 170 degrees.

Some processed pork products are cured or hot-smoked to USDA standards, which eliminates the danger of trichinosis, even without further cooking. Never assume, however, that *any* ham or sausage is safe to eat uncooked. Read the label carefully, or ask your butcher for this information if the product is not labeled.

Making Stock

Although canned chicken broth or stock is all right for emergencies, homemade chicken stock has a rich flavor that is hard to match. Moreover, the commercial broths—particularly the canned ones—are likely to be oversalted.

To make your own stock, save chicken parts as they accumulate and put them in a bag in the freezer; then have a rainy-day stock-making session, using the recipe below. The skin from a yellow onion will add color; the optional veal bone will add extra flavor and richness to the stock.

Basic Chicken Stock

3 pounds bony chicken parts, such as wings, back, and neck
1 veal knuckle (optional)
3 quarts cold water
1 yellow unpeeled onion, stuck with 2 cloves
2 stalks celery with leaves, cut in two
12 crushed peppercorns
2 carrots, scraped and cut into 2-inch lengths
4 sprigs parsley
1 bay leaf
1 tablespoon fresh thyme, or 1 teaspoon dried
Salt (optional)

1. Wash chicken parts and veal knuckle (if you are using it) and drain. Place in large soup kettle or stockpot (any big pot) with the remaining ingredients—except salt. Cover pot and bring to a boil over medium heat.
2. Lower heat and simmer stock, partly covered, 2 to 3 hours. Skim foam and scum from top of stock several times. Add salt to taste after stock has cooked 1 hour.
3. Strain stock through fine sieve placed over large bowl. Discard solids. Let stock cool uncovered (this will speed cooling process). When completely cool, refrigerate. Fat will rise and congeal conveniently at top. You may skim it off and discard it or leave it as a protective covering until ready to use.

Beef stock, although time-consuming to make, requires very little attention while cooking. Use marrow bones and an inexpensive cut of beef, such as shin, in roughly equal amounts. If you use beef knuckle, have the butcher saw it into quarters. During the first few minutes of cooking, the beef and bones will produce a scum that must be carefully removed from the surface, but for the bulk of the cooking time, the stock will require only occasional skimming. The cooking time given is approximate. Long, slow simmering is necessary to extract all the flavor from the ingredients, but a half hour more or less will not matter significantly. When the stock is cooked, leave it uncovered at room temperature until it is completely cool: Stock will turn sour if it is covered while still warm. Stock may be refrigerated for several days or frozen for up to three months.

Beef Stock

1 leek (optional)
2 medium-size carrots
3 to 4 celery stalks with leaves
6 to 8 sprigs fresh parsley
1½ teaspoons chopped fresh thyme or ½ to ¾ teaspoon dried
Large onion
3 cloves garlic (optional)
4 pounds shin of beef with bone
2 pounds marrow bones, or 1 pound marrow bones and 1 beef knuckle
1 bay leaf
6 whole cloves (optional)
8 peppercorns
1½ teaspoons salt

1. Trim and clean leek; peel carrots, wash celery and parsley; chop fresh thyme, if using. Do not peel onion and garlic.
2. Place beef and bones in kettle and add approximately 4 quarts of cold water, to cover beef and bones by about 2 inches. Over moderate heat, bring to a simmer, skimming off scum as it rises.
3. When scum has almost stopped surfacing, add vegetables, herbs, and seasonings and return to a simmer. Partially cover pot and, over low heat, cook stock at a gentle simmer, skimming as necessary, approximately 4 to 5 hours.
4. Taste stock. Cook down further if flavor needs to be intensified, or add water if it has reduced too much and the flavor is too strong.
5. Strain stock through fine sieve into large bowl or jar. Discard bones, meat, vegetables, and seasonings. Allow stock to cool completely, uncovered.
6. Refrigerate stock until a layer of fat has solidified on surface. Remove it with a spoon and discard it. Return defatted stock to refrigerator, or freeze, for future use.

In broiling, the food cooks directly under the heat source. In grilling, the food cooks either directly over an open fire or on a well-seasoned cast-iron or stoneware griddle placed directly over a burner. Lucy Wing broils Chinese butterflied pork (page 25).

Roasting and Baking

Roasting originally meant cooking on a spit over an open fire. It is a dry-heat process, usually used for large cuts of meat and poultry, that cooks the food by exposing it to heated air in an oven or, perhaps, a covered barbecue. For more even circulation of heat, the food should be placed in a shallow pan or on a rack in a pan. For greater moisture retention, baste the food with its own juices, fat, or a flavorful marinade.

Baking applies to the dry-heat cooking of foods such as casseroles; small cuts of meat, fish, poultry, and vegetables; and, of course, breads and pastries. Some foods are baked tightly covered to retain their juices and flavors; others, such as breads, cakes and cookies, are baked in open pans to release moisture. Meryle Evans's Menu 2 features spoonbreads baked in ramekins (page 71).

Pantry (for this volume)

A well-stocked, properly organized pantry is essential for preparing great meals in the shortest time possible. Whether your pantry consists of a small refrigerator and two or three shelves over the sink, or a large freezer, refrigerator, and entire room just off the kitchen, you must protect staples from heat and light.

In maintaining your pantry, follow these rules:

1. Store staples by kind and date. Canned goods, canisters, and spices need a separate shelf, or a separate spot on a shelf. Date all staples—shelved, refrigerated, or frozen—by writing the date directly on the package or on a bit of masking tape. Then put the oldest ones in front to be sure you use them first.

2. Store flour, sugar, and other dry ingredients in canisters or jars with tight lids. Glass and clear plastic allow you to see at a glance how much remains.

3. Keep a running grocery list so that you can note when a staple is half gone, and be sure to stock up.

ON THE SHELF:

Chilies, canned
jalapeños
mild green chilies
(Anaheim)

Cornstarch
Less likely to lump than flour, cornstarch is an excellent thickener for sauces. Substitute in the following proportions: 1 tablespoon cornstarch to 2 of flour.

Dried fruits
pitted prunes

Dried mushrooms
Imported from Asia and Europe, dried mushrooms provide rich flavor to cooked dishes. Stored airtight in a cool place they will keep up to a year.

Flour
all-purpose, bleached or unbleached
cornmeal
May be yellow or white and of various degrees of coarseness. The stone-ground variety, milled to retain the germ of the corn, generally has a superior flavor.

Garlic
Store in a cool, dry, well-ventilated place. Garlic powder and garlic salt are not adequate substitutes for fresh garlic.

Herbs and spices
The flavor of fresh herbs is much better than that of dried. Fresh herbs should be refrigerated and used as soon as possible. The following herbs are perfectly acceptable dried, but buy in small amounts, store airtight in dry area away from heat and light, and use as quickly as possible. In measuring herbs, remember that one part dried will equal three parts fresh. *Note:* Dried chives and parsley should not be on your shelf, since they have little or no flavor; frozen chives are acceptable. Buy whole spices rather than ground, as they keep their flavor much longer. Grind spices at home and store as directed for herbs.

basil
bay leaves
caraway seeds
cardamom, whole or ground
Cayenne pepper
cinnamon
cloves, whole and ground
coriander, whole and ground
cumin
dill
ginger
mustard
nutmeg, whole and ground
oregano
paprika
pepper
black peppercorns
These are unripe peppercorns dried in their husks. Grind with a pepper mill for each use.
white peppercorns
These are the same as the black variety, but are picked ripe and husked.

Use them in pale sauces when black pepper specks would spoil the appearance.
red pepper flakes (also called crushed red pepper)
rosemary
saffron
Made from the dried stigmas of a species of crocus, this spice—the most costly of all seasonings—adds both color and flavor. Use sparingly.
sage leaves
salt
Use coarse salt—commonly available as Kosher or sea—for its superior flavor, texture, and purity. Kosher salt and sea salt are less salty than table salt. Substitute in the following proportions: three-quarters teaspoon table salt equals just under one teaspoon Kosher or sea salt.
tarragon
thyme
turmeric

Honey

Nuts, whole, chopped, or slivered
pecans
pine nuts (pignoli)
walnuts

Oils
corn, safflower, peanut, or vegetable
Because these neutral-tasting oils have high smoking points, they are good for high-heat sautéing.

olive oil
Sample French, Greek, Spanish, and Italian oils. Olive oil ranges in color from pale yellow to dark green and in taste from mild and delicate to rich and fruity. Different olive oils can be used for different purposes: for example, lighter ones for cooking, stronger ones for salads. The finest quality olive oil is labeled extra-virgin or virgin.
sesame oil
Dark amber-colored Oriental-style oil, used for seasoning; do not substitute light cold-pressed sesame oil.
walnut oil
Rich and nutty tasting. It turns rancid easily, so keep it in a tightly closed container in the refrigerator.

Onions
Store all dry-skinned onions in a cool, dry, well-ventilated place.
red or Italian onions
Zesty tasting and generally eaten raw. The perfect salad onion.
shallots
The most subtle member of the onion family, the shallot has a delicate garlic flavor.
yellow onions
All-purpose cooking onions, strong in taste.

Potatoes, boiling and baking
"New" potatoes are not a particular kind of potato, but any potato that has not been stored.

Rice

long-grain white rice
  Slender grains, much longer than they are wide, that become light and fluffy when cooked and are best for general use.

Soy Sauce

Chinese
  Usually quite salty and richly flavored—for cooking.

Stock, chicken and beef
  For maximum flavor and quality, your own stock is best (see recipe page 13), but canned stock, or broth, is adequate for most recipes and convenient to have on hand.

Sugar

light brown sugar
granulated sugar

Tomatoes

Italian plum tomatoes
  Canned plum tomatoes (preferably imported) are an acceptable substitute for fresh.

Vinegars

red and white wine
  vinegars
rice wine vinegar
  A mild white Oriental vinegar
tarragon vinegar
  A white wine vinegar flavored with fresh tarragon, it is especially good in salads.

Wines and spirits

Madeira
Pernod
sherry, dry
red wine, dry
white wine, dry

IN THE REFRIGERATOR:

Basil
  Though fresh basil is widely available only in summer, try to use it whenever possible to replace dried; the flavor is markedly superior. Stand the stems, preferably with roots intact, in a jar of water, and loosely cover leaves with a plastic bag.

Bread crumbs
  You need never buy bread crumbs. To make fresh crumbs, use fresh or day-old bread and process in food processor or blender. For dried, toast bread 30 minutes in preheated 250-degree oven, turning occasionally to prevent slices from browning. Proceed as for fresh. Store bread crumbs in an airtight container: fresh crumbs in the refrigerator, and dried crumbs in a cool, dry place. Either type may also be frozen for several weeks if tightly wrapped in a plastic bag.

Butter

Many cooks prefer unsalted butter because of its finer flavor and because it does not burn as easily as salted.

Celery

Cheese

Cheddar cheese, sharp
  A firm cheese, ranging in color from nearly white to yellow. Cheddar is a versatile cooking cheese.

Gruyère
  This firm cheese resembles Swiss, but has smaller holes and a sharper flavor. A quality Gruyère will have a slight "gleam" in its eyes, or holes.

Parmesan cheese
  Avoid the pre-grated packaged variety; it is very expensive and almost flavorless. Buy Parmesan by the quarter- or half-pound wedge and grate as needed: 4 ounces produces about one cup of grated cheese.

Chives

Refrigerate fresh chives wrapped in plastic. You may also buy small pots of growing chives—keep them on a windowsill and snip as needed.

Coriander

Also called *cilantro* or Chinese parsley, its pungent leaves resemble flat-leaf parsley. Keep in a glass of water covered with a plastic bag.

Cream

half-and-half
heavy cream
light cream
sour cream
Crème fraîche, homemade or commercial (see recipe page 68)

Dill

Store fresh dill as you would coriander.

Eggs

Will keep 4 to 5 weeks in refrigerator. For best results, bring to room temperature before using, except when separating.

Ginger, fresh

Found in the produce section. Wrap in a paper towel, then in plastic, and refrigerate; it will keep for about 1 month, but should be checked weekly for mold. To preserve it longer, place the whole ginger root in a small sherry-filled jar; it will last almost indefinitely, although not without changes in the ginger. Or, if you prefer, store it in the freezer, where it will last about 3 months. Fresh, firm ginger need not be peeled.

Lemons

In addition to its many uses in cooking, a slice of lemon rubbed over cut apples and pears will keep them from discoloring. Do not substitute bottled juice or lemon extract.

Limes
Milk
Mint

Fresh mint will keep for a week if wrapped in a damp paper towel and enclosed in a plastic bag.

Mustards

The recipes in this book usually call for Dijon or coarse-grain mustard.

Parsley

The two most commonly available kinds of parsley are flat-leaf and curly; they can be used interchangeably when necessary. Flat-leaf parsley has a more distinctive flavor and is generally preferred in cooking. Curly parsley wilts less easily and is excellent for garnishing. Store parsley in a glass of water and cover loosely with a plastic bag. It will keep for a week in the refrigerator. Or wash and dry it, and refrigerate in a small plastic bag with a dry paper towel inside to absorb any moisture.

Scallions

Scallions have a mild onion flavor. Store wrapped in plastic.

Yogurt

Equipment

Proper cooking equipment makes the work light and is a good cook's most prized possession. You can cook expertly without a store-bought steamer or even a food processor, but basic pans, knives, and a few other items are indispensable. Below are the things you need—and some attractive options—for preparing the menus in this volume.

Pots and pans
Large kettle or stockpot
3 skillets (large, medium, small) with covers
2 heavy-gauge sauté pans, 10 to 12 inches in diameter, with covers
3 saucepans with covers (1-, 2-, and 4-quart capacities)
Choose heavy-gauge enameled cast-iron, plain cast-iron, aluminum-clad stainless steel, or aluminum (but you need at least one saucepan that is not aluminum). Best—but very expensive—is tin-lined copper.

Large flameproof casserole or Dutch oven with cover
Roasting pan with rack
2 shallow baking pans (13 x 9 x 2-inch, and 9 x 9-inch)
2 cookie sheets (11 x 17-inch and 15 x 10-inch)
9-inch pie pan
Large ovenproof baking dish
Heatproof serving platters
Four 10- to 12-ounce ramekins or individual soufflé dishes
Salad bowl

Knives
A carbon-steel knife takes a sharp edge but tends to rust. You must wash and dry it after each use; otherwise it can blacken foods and counter tops. Good-quality stainless steel knives, frequently honed, are less trouble and will serve just as well in the home kitchen. Never put a fine knife in the dishwasher. Rinse it, dry it, and put it away—but not loose in a drawer. Knives will stay sharp if they have their own storage rack.
Small paring knife
10-inch chef's knife
Bread knife (serrated edge)
Sharpening steel

Other cooking tools
2 sets of mixing bowls in graduated sizes, one set preferably glass or stainless steel

Colander with a round base (stainless steel, aluminum, or enamel)
2 sieves in fine and coarse mesh
2 strainers in fine and coarse mesh
2 sets of measuring cups and spoons in graduated sizes
One for dry ingredients, another for shortenings and liquids.
Cooking spoon
Slotted spoon
Long-handled wooden spoons
Wooden spatula (for stirring hot ingredients)
2 metal spatulas or turners (for lifting hot foods from pans)
Slotted spatula
Fork (for combining dry ingredients)
Rubber or vinyl spatula (for folding in ingredients)
Rolling pin
Grater (metal, with several sizes of holes)
A rotary grater is handy for hard cheese.
Small wire whisk
Balloon whisk
Pair of metal tongs
Wooden board
Instant-reading meat thermometer
Garlic press
Vegetable peeler
Mortar and pestle
Vegetable steamer
Pastry brush for basting (a small, new paintbrush that is not nylon serves well)
Vegetable brush
Cooling rack
Kitchen shears
Kitchen timer
Aluminum foil
Paper towels
Plastic wrap
Waxed paper
Thin rubber gloves
Oven mitts or potholders

Electric appliances
Food processor or blender
A blender will do most of the work required in this volume, but a food processor will do it more quickly and in larger volume. A food processor should be considered a necessity, not a luxury, for anyone who enjoys cooking.
Electric mixer

Optional cooking tools
Salad spinner
Butter warmer
Melon baller
Spice grinder
Apple corer
Salad servers
Citrus juicer
Inexpensive glass kind from the dime store will do.
Nutmeg grater
Zester
Roll of masking tape or white paper tape for labeling and dating

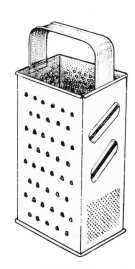

GRATER

COLANDER

STRAINER

FOOD
PROCESSOR

RUBBER
SPATULA

MIXING BOWLS

SLOTTED
SPATULA

METAL
SPATULA

WHISK

SHARPENING STEEL

CHEF'S KNIFE

PARING KNIFE

VEGETABLE STEAMER

CASSEROLE

SAUCEPANS

SAUTÉ PAN

SKILLET

Lucy Wing

MENU 1 (Right)
Thai Pork with Coriander and Garlic Chives
Braised Red Bell Pepper and Eggplant
Steamed Rice
Tropical Fruit Salad

MENU 2
Indonesian Pork Satay
Golden Rice
Vegetables with Peanut Sauce

MENU 3
Broiled Chinese Butterflied Pork
Sesame Noodles
Stir-Fried Broccoli
Honeydew with Crystallized Ginger

Although Lucy Wing grew up eating traditional Chinese food, she describes herself as an eclectic cook with an international palate. "I particularly enjoy simplifying recipes from many lands and experimenting with exotic ingredients," she says, "and I like to cook quickly to preserve the natural flavors of the food." The three Asian menus she presents here are all easy to prepare and are distinguished by their unusual seasonings and dramatic colors.

Menu 1 offers Thai dishes. The cook marinates thin slices of pork loin in a sauce flavored with coriander roots and garlic chives, then browns the pork quickly in a wok. Braised red bell pepper and eggplant strips and steamed rice accompany the pork.

In Menu 2, she prepares Indonesia's national dish, *satay*, in which marinated cubes of meat are threaded on bamboo skewers and then grilled. Every one of Indonesia's thousands of islands has its own version of *satay*, but only the Hindu island of Bali serves pork *satay* (all of the other islands are Islamic). Rice flavored with coconut and turmeric (*nasi kuning*), and vegetables with peanut sauce (*gado-gado*) are the colorful side dishes.

Chinese specialties make up Menu 3: broiled pork, stir-fried broccoli, and sesame noodles. Traditionally the Chinese marinate the pork for this dish for several hours, then roast it for another hour. Lucy Wing's streamlined version uses already-tender boneless pork loin, which is broiled for about 25 minutes.

Lightly browned slices of pork loin are garnished with fresh coriander and served with braised vegetables and fluffy steamed rice for this company meal. Offer the tropical fruits on individual plates or in a large bowl.

Thai Pork with Coriander and Garlic Chives
Braised Red Bell Pepper and Eggplant / Steamed Rice
Tropical Fruit Salad

Coriander roots and garlic chives flavor the sauce for the pork. Garlic chives, also called Chinese chives, are more strongly flavored than the Western type and somewhat garlicky. The narrow, flat leaves are cut to about 8 inches long and sold in bunches in Chinese and Japanese markets. Sometimes you will find them with small white flower heads intact; these are edible as well.

The eggplant dish calls for *nam pla*, a Thai sauce made from fermented fish. (Southeast Asians often use fish sauce in place of salt.) You may omit the *nam pla*, but if you do, increase the soy sauce as indicated.

WHAT TO DRINK

The cook suggests a piña colada as a refreshing accompaniment to this menu. If you prefer wine, choose a California Pinot Blanc or Alsatian Sylvaner.

SHOPPING LIST AND STAPLES

2-pound boneless center pork loin roast, trimmed
Large eggplant (about 1½ pounds)
Medium-size red bell pepper
Medium-size bunch coriander with roots
Large bunch garlic chives, or small bunch scallions
Large clove garlic
Small ripe pineapple
Medium-size ripe mango or papaya (about 1 pound)
1 kiwi
2 small or 4 tiny bananas
¾ cup peanut or vegetable oil
12-ounce bottle nam pla, Thai fish sauce, or other Oriental fish sauce (optional)
2 or 3 tablespoons light soy sauce, preferably Chinese
1 cup long-grain rice
4 teaspoons sugar
1 tablespoon plus 2 teaspoons cornstarch
½ teaspoon ground ginger
Dash of crushed red pepper
Salt and freshly ground pepper

UTENSILS

Large wok or Dutch oven
Large skillet with cover
2 large saucepans, 1 with cover
Large bowl
Medium-size bowl
Small bowl
Strainer
Measuring cups and spoons
Chef's knife
Paring knife
Slotted spoon
2 wooden spoons
Rubber spatula
Vegetable peeler

START-TO-FINISH STEPS

One hour ahead: Place pineapple, mango, or papaya if using, and kiwi in coldest part of refrigerator to chill.

1. Follow rice recipe step 1 and pork recipe steps 1 and 2.
2. Follow rice recipe step 2 and pork recipe steps 3 and 4.
3. Follow eggplant recipe steps 1 and 2.
4. Follow fruit salad recipe steps 1 and 2.
5. Follow eggplant recipe steps 3 and 4.
6. Follow rice recipe step 3.
7. Follow pork recipe steps 5 through 7, rice recipe step 4, and serve with eggplant.
8. For dessert, follow fruit salad recipe steps 3 and 4.

RECIPES

Thai Pork with Coriander and Garlic Chives

Large bunch garlic chives, or small bunch scallions
Medium-size bunch coriander with roots
Large clove garlic
2-pound boneless center pork loin roast, trimmed
2 teaspoons salt
2 teaspoons sugar
2 teaspoons cornstarch
Freshly ground pepper
½ cup peanut or vegetable oil

1. Preheat oven to 200 degrees. Place 4 dinner plates in oven to warm.
2. Rinse garlic chives and coriander, and dry with paper towels. Cut enough garlic chives into 1½-inch lengths to measure ½ cup. Cut off coriander roots and chop enough to measure 1 tablespoon. Reserve coriander leaves for garnish. Peel garlic and mince enough to measure 1 tablespoon.
3. Cut pork crosswise into 2 x 3 x ¼-inch-thick slices.

4. In large bowl, combine chopped coriander roots, garlic, salt, sugar, cornstarch, pepper to taste, and ¼ cup oil. Add pork, toss until coated, and set aside 10 minutes.

5. In large wok or Dutch oven, heat the remaining oil over medium-high heat until it begins to sizzle. Add half the pork and sauté, stirring occasionally, until lightly browned, 3 to 4 minutes. Transfer pork to a plate and cover loosely with foil to keep warm. Sauté remaining pork until lightly browned.

6. Return first half of pork to wok and stir together. Warm pork briefly, about 30 seconds, stirring constantly. Add garlic chives and stir to combine.

7. Divide pork among 4 warm dinner plates and garnish with coriander leaves.

Braised Red Bell Pepper and Eggplant

Large eggplant (about 1½ pounds)
Medium-size red bell pepper
1 tablespoon cornstarch
2 teaspoons sugar
Dash of crushed red pepper
½ teaspoon ground ginger
2 or 3 tablespoons light soy sauce, preferably Chinese
1 tablespoon nam pla, Thai fish sauce, or other Oriental fish sauce (optional)
¼ cup peanut or vegetable oil

1. Rinse eggplant and red bell pepper, and dry with paper towels. Trim eggplant and cut into 3 x ½ x ½-inch-thick strips. Halve bell pepper, core, seed, remove membranes, and cut into ¼-inch-thick strips.

2. In small bowl, combine cornstarch, sugar, crushed red pepper, ginger, 2 tablespoons soy sauce and 1 tablespoon nam pla, if using, or 3 tablespoons soy sauce. Stir mixture until blended and set aside.

3. In large skillet, heat oil over medium-high heat until hot. Add eggplant and pepper strips, and sauté, stirring constantly, until vegetables begin to wilt, 3 to 4 minutes.

4. Stir cornstarch mixture to recombine and pour over vegetables, tossing until thoroughly combined. Reduce heat to low, cover skillet, and cook, stirring occasionally, about 5 minutes, or until eggplant is tender. Remove from heat and keep covered until ready to serve.

Steamed Rice

1 cup long-grain rice

1. In large saucepan, bring 6 cups water to a boil over high heat.

2. Add rice and stir. Keeping liquid at a boil, cook rice uncovered, stirring occasionally, until tender, about 20 minutes.

3. Just before rice is done, bring about 1 inch of water to a boil in another saucepan. Turn rice into strainer and place over pan of water, making sure bottom of strainer does not touch boiling water. Cover pan and allow rice to steam until ready to serve.

4. Fluff rice with fork and divide among dinner plates.

Tropical Fruit Salad

Small ripe pineapple, chilled
1 kiwi, chilled
Medium-size ripe mango or papaya (about 1 pound), chilled
2 small or 4 tiny bananas

1. Remove stem, then halve pineapple lengthwise; reserve one half for another use. Quarter remaining half lengthwise, core each quarter, and cut flesh away from rind with paring knife. Remove pineapple eyes, cut each quarter into spears, and place in medium-size bowl.

2. Peel kiwi, quarter, and cut into bite-size pieces. Add to bowl. Peel mango: Using chef's knife, make 4 or more evenly spaced lengthwise cuts through mango flesh, pressing knife against pit; then score firmly several times crosswise and gently dislodge mango pieces with point of knife. Discard pit. Add mango pieces to bowl, cover with plastic wrap, and refrigerate.

3. Just before serving, peel bananas. Cut small bananas crosswise into bite-size slices, or, if using tiny bananas, leave whole. Remove fruit from refrigerator and add bananas.

4. Divide fruit salad among 4 salad plates and serve.

ADDED TOUCH

Canned coconut milk is readily available in Oriental markets and well-stocked supermarkets.

Coconut Chicken Curry Soup

1 chicken breast half (about ½ pound)
Small onion
1 tablespoon peanut or vegetable oil
1 teaspoon cornstarch
1 teaspoon curry powder, approximately
½ teaspoon salt
1 cup canned unsweetened coconut milk

1. In medium-size saucepan, bring chicken breast half and 1½ cups water to a boil over high heat. Cover, reduce heat to low, and cook until chicken is fork tender and flesh is white throughout, about 15 minutes.

2. Meanwhile, peel onion and chop enough to measure ½ cup.

3. Drain chicken, reserving stock; wipe out pan with paper towels. Remove skin and bone from chicken, cut meat into ½-inch cubes, place on plate, and cover with foil to keep warm.

4. In dry saucepan, heat oil over medium heat. Add onion and cook, stirring frequently, 4 to 5 minutes, or until soft.

5. Add cornstarch, 1 teaspoon curry powder or slightly more, if desired, and salt; cook 1 minute, stirring until blended.

6. Add coconut milk and 1 cup reserved chicken stock to pan, and cook soup over medium heat, stirring until slightly thickened, 3 to 4 minutes.

7. Add cubed chicken to soup, stir, and heat through, about 1 minute.

8. Divide soup among 4 bowls and serve immediately.

Indonesian Pork Satay
Golden Rice
Vegetables with Peanut Sauce

Crisscross skewers of pork in the center of each plate, then mound the rice and vegetables with peanut sauce on either side.

Chinese green beans and Napa cabbage are two common Oriental vegetables. Similar in taste and color to the American green bean, the Chinese variety usually measures 12 inches long and has a slightly chewy texture. Napa cabbage has an oblong head of broad, frilled, pale green leaves and a delicate flavor. Both are available year-round in many supermarkets and Chinese groceries.

WHAT TO DRINK

Ice-cold beer or ale is a good partner for these dishes, or try an India Pale ale for an interesting change of pace.

SHOPPING LIST AND STAPLES

2-pound boneless blade Boston pork roast
Medium-size head Napa cabbage (about 1½ pounds)
3 medium-size carrots (about ¾ pound total weight)
½ pound Chinese green beans or regular green beans
Small onion
Medium-size clove garlic
Small lemon
1¾ cups chicken stock, preferably homemade (see page 13), or canned
3 tablespoons peanut or vegetable oil

1 tablespoon rice wine vinegar or white wine vinegar
5 tablespoons light soy sauce, preferably Chinese
6-ounce jar creamy peanut butter
1 cup long-grain rice
2 tablespoons sugar
6-ounce package unsweetened shredded coconut
1 teaspoon ground coriander
1 teaspoon ground ginger
½ teaspoon turmeric
Dash of crushed red pepper
Salt

UTENSILS

Large skillet with cover
Medium-size saucepan with cover
Small heavy-gauge saucepan
Large bowl
2 large platters
Colander
Measuring cups and spoons
Chef's knife
Paring knife
Wooden spoon
Slotted spoon
Pastry brush
Vegetable peeler
Eight 10-inch bamboo skewers

START-TO-FINISH STEPS

1. Follow pork recipe steps 1 through 3.
2. Follow rice recipe steps 1 and 2.
3. Follow pork recipe steps 4 and 5.
4. Meanwhile, remove rice from heat and follow vegetables recipe steps 1 through 9.
5. Follow rice recipe step 3 and serve with pork and vegetables with peanut sauce.

RECIPES

Indonesian Pork Satay

2-pound boneless blade Boston pork roast
2 teaspoons minced garlic
¼ cup light soy sauce, preferably Chinese
1 tablespoon rice wine vinegar or white wine vinegar
1 tablespoon peanut or vegetable oil
2 tablespoons sugar
1 teaspoon ground coriander
1 teaspoon ground ginger
1 teaspoon salt

1. Cut pork into 1-inch cubes.
2. In large bowl, blend all ingredients except pork. Add pork, stir until evenly coated, and set aside 15 minutes.
3. Preheat broiler.
4. Using slotted spoon, transfer pork to large platter, reserving marinade. Divide pork evenly among 8 skewers

and place on rack in foil-lined broiler pan.
5. Broil meat 6 to 7 inches from heat source, turning skewers occasionally and brushing pork with marinade, until meat is a rich brown, about 20 minutes.

Golden Rice

2 tablespoons peanut or vegetable oil
½ cup chopped onion
1 cup long-grain rice
½ teaspoon salt
½ teaspoon turmeric
⅓ to ½ cup unsweetened shredded coconut
1¾ cups chicken stock

1. In medium-size saucepan, heat oil over medium-high heat. Add onion and sauté, stirring occasionally, until lightly browned, about 2 minutes. Stir in rice, salt, turmeric, and coconut to taste. Add chicken stock, stir, and bring to a boil over high heat.
2. Cover pan, reduce heat to low, and simmer rice until tender, about 20 minutes. Stir rice once with fork while cooking. Keep covered until ready to serve.
3. Fluff rice with fork and divide among 4 dinner plates.

Vegetables with Peanut Sauce

3 medium-size carrots (about ¾ pound total weight)
½ pound Chinese green beans or regular green beans
Medium-size head Napa cabbage (about 1½ pounds)
¼ cup creamy peanut butter
1 tablespoon light soy sauce, preferably Chinese
2 teaspoons lemon juice
Dash of crushed red pepper

1. Peel carrots, trim, and cut into ⅛-inch-thick rounds.
2. In large skillet, bring ½ inch water to a boil over medium-high heat. Add carrots, cover, and cook until crisp-tender, 3 or 4 minutes.
3. Meanwhile, trim stem ends of beans and cut enough beans into 2-inch lengths to measure about 2 cups.
4. Using slotted spoon, transfer cooked carrots to a large platter, leaving water at a boil. Cover carrots loosely with foil to keep warm. Place beans in boiling water, cover, and cook until crisp-tender, 3 or 4 minutes.
5. While beans are cooking, cut cabbage in half, reserving one half for another use. Cut remaining half crosswise into ½-inch-wide slices; wash and drain in colander.
6. Transfer cooked beans from pan to platter, keeping them separate from carrots. Keep water in pan at a boil.
7. Place cabbage in boiling water, cover, and cook just until wilted, about 1 minute. Turn cabbage into colander, drain, and transfer to platter with carrots and beans. Keep vegetables covered with foil.
8. Combine peanut butter, soy sauce, lemon juice, and red pepper in small heavy-gauge saucepan, and cook over low heat, stirring constantly, until sauce is smooth and creamy, about 2 minutes.
9. Divide vegetables among dinner plates, top with peanut sauce, and serve with remaining sauce.

Broiled Chinese Butterflied Pork / Sesame Noodles
Stir-Fried Broccoli
Honeydew with Crystallized Ginger

For an easy buffet, present the glazed pork on the same platter as the sesame noodles, and serve the stir-fried broccoli separately. Chilled honeydew wedges sprinkled with crystallized ginger are the dessert.

V isit the Oriental food section of your supermarket or an Oriental grocery to stock up on the ingredients for this menu. Rich, mahogany-colored *hoisin* sauce is a sweet-pungent mixture made with soybeans, ground chilies, garlic, and spices, which is often used in China as a condiment. *Hoisin* sauce is sold in cans or jars; any unused sauce can be stored in a covered jar in the refrigerator, where it will keep for several months. There are no substitutes.

WHAT TO DRINK

Tea, whether fresh-brewed or iced, is the time-honored drink to have with a Chinese meal. Well-chilled Chinese beer would also be very satisfying.

SHOPPING LIST AND STAPLES

2-pound boneless pork loin top loin roast, butterflied
1 bunch Chinese broccoli, preferably, or regular broccoli (1¼ pounds)
½ pound medium-size mushrooms
Large onion
Small bunch scallions for garnish (optional)
2 large cloves garlic
1 honeydew melon (about 4 pounds), or 1 cantaloupe (about 2 pounds)
Large lime (optional)
2 tablespoons peanut or vegetable oil
8-ounce bottle Chinese sesame oil
⅔ cup catsup
15-ounce jar hoisin sauce
12-ounce jar sesame paste (tahini), or 3 tablespoons creamy peanut butter
10-ounce bottle light soy sauce, preferably Chinese
9-ounce bottle oyster sauce
½ pound fresh Chinese egg noodles, or dry spaghetti, spaghettini, or vermicelli
1 teaspoon sugar
4¼-ounce package crystallized ginger
Dash of crushed red pepper
Salt
1 tablespoon dry sherry

UTENSILS

Large skillet

Large saucepan
Small saucepan
Small bowl
Colander
Measuring cups and spoons
Chef's knife
Paring knife
Wooden spoon
Wok spatula (optional)
Pastry brush
Cutting board

START-TO-FINISH STEPS

1. Follow pork recipe step 1 and noodles recipe step 1.
2. Follow honeydew recipe step 1.
3. Follow noodles recipe steps 2 through 4.
4. Follow pork recipe steps 2 and 3.
5. Follow broccoli recipe steps 1 through 3.
6. Follow pork recipe step 4 and broccoli recipe steps 4 through 6.
7. Follow pork recipe step 5, noodles recipe step 5, and serve with broccoli.
8. For dessert, follow honeydew recipe step 2.

RECIPES

Broiled Chinese Butterflied Pork

2-pound boneless pork loin top loin roast, butterflied
2 tablespoons minced garlic
⅔ cup catsup
⅓ cup hoisin sauce
1 tablespoon light soy sauce, preferably Chinese
1 tablespoon dry sherry
½ teaspoon salt

1. Preheat broiler.
2. Open loin, spread out to resemble butterfly wings, and press gently to flatten. Place pork on rack in broiling pan and place pan in broiler. Broil meat 6 inches from heat source, turning occasionally, about 20 minutes.
3. Meanwhile, make sauce for glazing: In small saucepan, combine remaining ingredients and bring to a boil over medium-low heat. Stir sauce and turn heat down as low as possible.
4. Brush pork with sauce and continue to broil, basting with sauce and turning, until completely glazed, 3 to 4 minutes. Transfer pork to serving platter and cover loosely with foil to keep warm.
5. When ready to serve, carve 4 or more slices of pork and transfer to platter. Serve remaining sauce separately.

Sesame Noodles

½ pound fresh Chinese egg noodles, or dry spaghetti, spaghettini, or vermicelli
2 tablespoons finely chopped scallions (optional)
3 tablespoons sesame paste (tahini) or creamy peanut butter

3 tablespoons light soy sauce, preferably Chinese
2 tablespoons Chinese sesame oil
Dash of crushed red pepper

1. In large saucepan, bring 3 to 4 quarts water to a boil over high heat.
2. Place noodles in boiling water and cook until just tender, 2 to 5 minutes.
3. Meanwhile, blend remaining ingredients with 2 tablespoons water in small bowl.
4. Turn noodles into colander to drain and then return to warm saucepan. Add sesame sauce, toss noodles until evenly coated, and set aside to cool to room temperature.
5. Just before serving, toss again, and transfer to serving platter. Garnish with scallions, if desired.

Stir-Fried Broccoli

1 bunch Chinese broccoli, preferably, or regular broccoli, (1¼ pounds)
Large onion
½ pound medium-size mushrooms
2 tablespoons peanut or vegetable oil
¼ cup oyster sauce
1 teaspoon sugar
Salt

1. Wash broccoli and dry with paper towels. Remove florets and any large leaves, and set aside. Cut stems diagonally into 1- to 1½-inch lengths.
2. Peel onion, slice thinly, and separate into rings. Wipe mushrooms with damp paper towels and cut into ¼-inch-thick slices.
3. Bring ½ inch water to a boil in large skillet over medium-high heat. Add broccoli stems and cook about 2 minutes, or until almost tender. Add florets and leaves and cook another 30 seconds. Turn broccoli into colander to drain; dry skillet.
4. Heat oil in skillet over medium-high heat. Add onions and stir fry just until wilted, about 2 minutes.
5. Add mushrooms to skillet and stir fry until tender, about 1 minute.
6. Stir in broccoli, oyster sauce, sugar, and salt to taste, and stir fry mixture just until heated through, about 2 minutes. Transfer to serving platter and cover loosely with foil to keep warm.

Honeydew with Crystallized Ginger

1 honeydew melon (about 4 pounds) or cantaloupe (about 2 pounds)
2½ tablespoons finely chopped crystallized ginger
1 lime for garnish, thinly sliced (optional)

1. Cut honeydew in half, reserving one half for another use. Remove seeds from remaining half and cut lengthwise into 4 wedges; remove rinds. Place wedges on serving platter, sprinkle with ginger, cover, and refrigerate.
2. Just before serving, remove melon from refrigerator and garnish platter with lime slices, if desired.

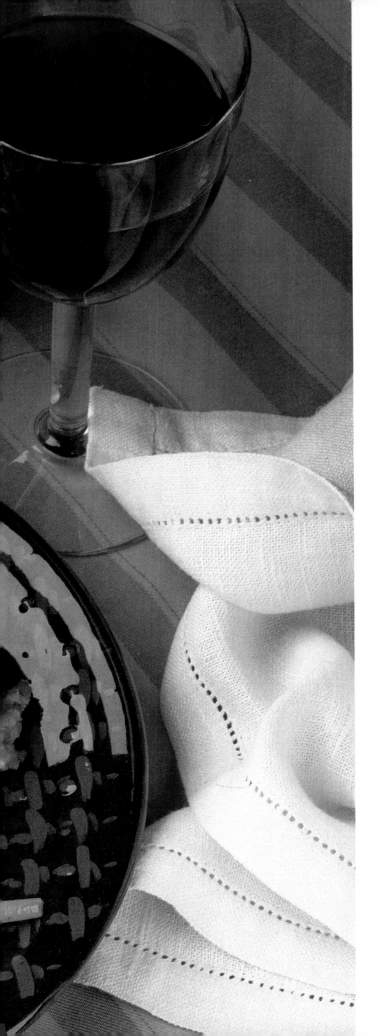

Holly Garrison

According to Holly Garrison, there have been three major influences on her cooking style: the Pennsylvania Dutch country where she spent her childhood; her southern grandmother and mother; and her father, who worked with the French diplomatic corps in the United States and gave her an appreciation of French food at an early age. Her three menus reflect these influences.

In Menu 1 she re-creates a meal reminiscent of Pennsylvania Dutch cooking. Hollowed-out Golden Delicious apples are stuffed with a sweet-and-sour combination of ground pork, sausage, seasonings, and apple cider. She serves the stuffed apples with green beans and mushrooms, and offers French bread slices spread with walnut-garlic butter on the side.

Menu 3 begins with sweet corn soup (ideally made from freshly picked corn), followed by Virginia's famous Smithfield ham, sliced and sautéed with zucchini, jícama, and red bell pepper. Tangy Cheddar cheese biscuits complete this festive dinner.

In Menu 2, Holly Garrison modifies a dish often eaten in Alsace in northeastern France—*choucroute garnie,* or sauerkraut garnished with sausage and pork. She lends an American touch to the meal by adding fruity California wine and a Red Delicious apple to the *choucroute* and serving roasted yams as an accompaniment.

Golden Delicious apples filled with lean ground pork, mild pork sausage, and bread crumbs make a substantial entrée. Serve the green beans and sautéed shiitake mushrooms with the apples, and the French bread warm from the oven.

27

Pork-and-Sausage-Stuffed Golden Apples
Green Bean and Mushroom Sauté
French Bread with Walnut-Garlic Butter

Golden Delicious apples work best here because they retain their shape and texture during baking. You can substitute Rome Beauties, although Golden Delicious are generally available all year round. To prepare this meal within an hour, stuff the apples first and, as they bake, prepare the rest of the meal.

Fresh Japanese *shiitake* mushrooms are sold at specialty food shops and some supermarkets specializing in imported delicacies. Discard their tough stems or reserve them for flavoring vegetable soups or meat stocks. As an alternative, you can use fresh golden oak mushrooms, a member of the *shiitake* family. If fresh mushrooms are unavailable, use dried *shiitake*.

WHAT TO DRINK

Try a light, fruity red wine with this menu. A good choice would be a French Beaujolais or Beaujolais-Villages.

SHOPPING LIST AND STAPLES

1 pound lean ground fresh pork
½ pound mild fresh pork sausage or link sausages
1 pound green beans
¼ pound fresh shiitake or other cultivated mushrooms, or ¼ pound dried shiitake
Small onion
2 small cloves garlic
Small bunch parsley
4 Golden Delicious apples (each about ½ pound)
Small red apple for garnish (optional)
Large lemon
1 stick plus 1 tablespoon unsalted butter
1 cup apple cider
11½-ounce bottle walnut oil, or 3 tablespoons vegetable oil
2 slices home-style white bread
1 long loaf French bread
4-ounce can walnut halves or pieces
1 teaspoon dried sage
Salt and freshly ground pepper

UTENSILS

Food processor or blender
2 large skillets, or 1 large skillet and 1 large wok
Medium-size saucepan
8 x 8-inch baking dish
Large bowl
Medium-size bowl
Small bowl
Colander
Measuring cups and spoons
Chef's knife
Paring knife
Wooden spoon
Slotted spoon
Teaspoon
Metal spatula
Juicer (optional)
Garlic press
Pastry brush
Apple corer (optional)

START-TO-FINISH STEPS

Thirty minutes ahead: Follow sauté recipe step 1 and bread recipe step 1.

1. Peel garlic cloves and set aside. Juice lemon for apples and sauté recipes.
2. Follow apples recipe steps 1 through 8.
3. Follow sauté recipe steps 2 through 5.
4. Follow bread recipe steps 2 through 4.
5. Follow apples recipe step 9 and bread recipe step 5.
6. Follow sauté recipe step 6.
7. Follow sauté recipe steps 7 and 8, apples recipe step 10, and serve with bread.

RECIPES

Pork-and-Sausage-Stuffed Golden Apples

Small onion
2 slices home-style white bread
Small bunch parsley
½ pound mild fresh pork sausage or link sausages
1 pound lean ground fresh pork
4 Golden Delicious apples (each about ½ pound)
Small red apple for garnish (optional)
¼ cup lemon juice plus 1 teaspoon (optional)
1 teaspoon dried sage
½ teaspoon salt
Freshly ground pepper
1 cup apple cider

1. Preheat oven to 350 degrees.
2. Peel and finely chop enough onion to measure ½ cup. Tear bread into pieces and process in blender to make about 1 cup crumbs. Rinse, dry, and chop enough parsley to measure ¼ cup, reserving 4 sprigs for garnish, if desired.
3. If using link sausages, remove from casings and cut into small pieces. In large skillet, cook sausage and pork over medium heat, stirring well with wooden spoon, 5 to 7 minutes, or until no trace of pink remains. With slotted spoon, transfer to large bowl.
4. Add onion to fat remaining in skillet and cook over medium heat, stirring until softened, about 3 minutes. Add onion to pork and sausage.
5. Wash and dry apples. Set aside red apple, if using, for garnish. With apple corer or paring knife, remove cores from whole yellow apples. Cut a thin slice from top of each apple. With paring knife and teaspoon, carefully hollow out apples, leaving ¼-inch-thick shell. Reserve pulp for stuffing mixture. Brush inside of each shell with lemon juice to prevent discoloration. Place apples in baking dish, spacing evenly.
6. Coarsely chop reserved apple pulp. Reserving 1 teaspoon, combine remaining lemon juice and pulp in small bowl. Add pulp mixture, bread crumbs, parsley, sage, salt, and pepper to taste, to skillet with pork and sausage and stir to combine.
7. Fill each apple with stuffing, mounding slightly. Place remaining stuffing around apples in baking dish; baste with a little apple cider.
8. Place apples in oven and bake 40 minutes, basting with cider about every 10 minutes.
9. Just before apples are done, halve red apple, if using, for garnish, reserving one half for another use. Core remaining half, cut into 4 thin wedges, and brush with reserved lemon juice.
10. Using spatula, carefully transfer apples from baking dish to 4 dinner plates and divide remaining stuffing among plates. Top each serving with a red apple wedge and parsley sprig, if desired. Serve immediately.

Green Bean and Mushroom Sauté

¼ pound fresh shiitake or other cultivated mushrooms, or ¼ pound dried shiitake
Salt
1 pound green beans
3 tablespoons unsalted butter
3 tablespoons walnut or vegetable oil
Small clove garlic, peeled
1 tablespoon lemon juice
Freshly ground pepper

1. If using dried shiitake, place in medium-size bowl with enough water to cover and set aside 20 to 30 minutes to soak.
2. In medium-size saucepan, bring 2½ quarts water and 2½ teaspoons salt to a boil over high heat.
3. Meanwhile, trim green beans and rinse in cold water. Place beans in boiling water and cook until crisp-tender, about 3 minutes.
4. Turn beans into colander, refresh under cold running water, and set aside to drain.
5. Remove mushroom stems, reserving for another use, and wipe caps with damp paper towels. Or, drain reconstituted shiitake and strain soaking liquid, reserving for another use; dry with paper towels and trim stems. Cut mushrooms into ¼-inch-thick slices.
6. In large skillet or wok, heat butter and oil over medium-high heat. When butter-oil mixture is hot, put garlic through press directly into pan. Add beans and mushrooms, and sauté, stirring, until mushrooms are limp and beans are hot and just tender, about 3 minutes.
7. Add lemon juice and salt and pepper to taste, tossing to combine.
8. Divide vegetable sauté among 4 dinner plates.

French Bread with Walnut-Garlic Butter

6 tablespoons unsalted butter
1 cup walnut halves or pieces
Small clove garlic, peeled
1 long loaf French bread

1. Cut 6 tablespoons butter into small pieces and set aside in small bowl to soften.
2. Coarsely chop walnuts in food processor fitted with steel blade or in blender.
3. Put garlic through press, stirring into softened butter to blend. Add walnuts and mix.
4. Cut bread in half lengthwise and spread each half with butter mixture. Place buttered halves together and wrap loaf in aluminum foil. Bake loaf in 350-degree oven about 20 minutes.
5. Just before serving, remove foil, cut bread crosswise into 4 pieces, and place in napkin-lined basket.

American Choucroute Garnie
Pan-Roasted Yams
Beet and Lettuce Salad with Mustard Vinaigrette

Colorful yams brighten a plate of pork loin, Polish sausage, and sauerkraut. Offer the beet and lettuce salad separately.

For the American *choucroute garnie*, buy a smoked center loin pork roast and have it prepared by your butcher for easy slicing into chops. Because this dish is quite salty, rinse the sauerkraut to remove its brine before cooking. If you wish to reduce the saltiness further, simmer the loin roast in water for about 20 minutes and drain before adding it to the sauerkraut. To add a slightly sweet flavor of anise to the pork, use the caraway seeds. Pungent mustard would be fitting with this entrée.

WHAT TO DRINK

This hearty menu deserves a lightly chilled California or Alsatian Riesling or Gewürztraminer. You can also use either type of wine in preparing the *choucroute garnie*.

SHOPPING LIST AND STAPLES

Smoked center loin pork roast (2½ to 3 pounds), chine bone sawed so roast carves easily
½ pound precooked kielbasa
4 yams (about 2½ pounds total weight)
Small head Bibb lettuce
Small head Boston lettuce
Small bunch arugula
4 small beets
Medium-size onion
Large clove garlic
Large Red Delicious apple
Large lemon, or ¼ cup white wine vinegar
Large egg
2 tablespoons unsalted butter
1 pound sauerkraut
¾ cup olive oil or vegetable oil, plus vegetable oil for pan roasting
2 tablespoons Dijon mustard
1 or 2 teaspoons caraway seeds (optional)
Coarse (kosher) salt (optional)
Salt
Freshly ground pepper
½ cup California Riesling or other fruity white wine

UTENSILS

Food processor or blender
12 x 9-inch roasting pan or ovenproof baking dish
4-quart enameled Dutch oven or heavy-gauge nonaluminum pan with tight-fitting cover
Medium-size saucepan with cover
Medium-size bowl plus additional bowl (optional)
Colander
Salad spinner (optional)
Measuring cups and spoons
Chef's knife
Paring knife
Wooden spoon
Metal tongs
Juicer

Vegetable peeler
Rolling pin (if using caraway seeds)

START-TO-FINISH STEPS

1. Follow yams recipe step 1 and salad recipe steps 1 and 2.
2. Follow choucroute recipe steps 1 through 3.
3. Follow yams recipe steps 2 through 4.
4. Follow vinaigrette recipe steps 1 and 2.
5. Follow salad recipe step 3 and turn yams.
6. Follow vinaigrette recipe step 3 and salad recipe step 4.
7. Follow choucroute recipe step 4, yams recipe step 5, and serve with salad.

RECIPES

American Choucroute Garnie

1 pound sauerkraut
½ pound precooked kielbasa
Medium-size onion
Large Red Delicious apple
1 or 2 teaspoons caraway seeds (optional)
2 tablespoons unsalted butter
Freshly ground pepper
½ cup California Riesling or other fruity white wine
Smoked center loin pork roast (2½ to 3 pounds), chine bone sawed so roast carves easily

1. Place sauerkraut in colander to drain. Cut kielbasa into ½-inch-thick slices and set aside. Peel and chop enough onion to measure 1 cup. Wash and dry apple. Halve, core, and coarsely chop enough apple to measure 1½ cups. Place caraway seeds, if using, between 2 sheets of waxed paper and crush with rolling pin.
2. Melt butter over medium heat in Dutch oven. When butter is bubbly, add onion and cook, stirring, until onion is softened, about 3 minutes. Stir in drained sauerkraut, caraway seeds, if using, pepper to taste, and wine.
3. Add pork to sauerkraut mixture and surround with kielbasa slices. Cover tightly, reduce heat to medium-low, and cook 45 minutes, or until pork is fork tender.
4. Transfer pork to cutting surface and slice into 4 chops. Divide among dinner plates and top each serving with sauerkraut and kielbasa slices.

Pan-Roasted Yams

4 yams (about 2½ pounds total weight)
Vegetable oil
Coarse (kosher) salt (optional)

1. Preheat oven to 375 degrees.
2. Peel yams and cut crosswise into 2-inch-thick pieces.
3. Pour vegetable oil about ¼-inch deep into roasting pan or ovenproof baking dish. Add yams and turn to coat with oil. Sprinkle with coarse salt, if desired.
4. Bake yams, turning once with tongs after 25 minutes, until tender and lightly browned, about 40 minutes.
5. Divide yams among 4 dinner plates.

Beet and Lettuce Salad with Mustard Vinaigrette

4 small beets
Small head Bibb lettuce
Small head Boston lettuce
Small bunch arugula
Mustard Vinaigrette (see following recipe)

1. Remove beet tops, leaving about 1-inch of stems. Wash beets and drain in colander. Place beets in medium-size saucepan, cover with water, and bring to a boil over medium-high heat. Reduce heat and simmer beets 30 minutes, or until tender when tested gently with point of knife. (Do not test beets too often or color will bleed.)
2. Meanwhile, separate lettuce leaves; wash lettuce and arugula, and dry in salad spinner or with paper towels. Trim off arugula stems and place greens in medium-size bowl. Cover with plastic wrap and refrigerate until ready to use.
3. When beets are cooked, turn into colander and refresh under cold running water; slip skins off with your fingers. Trim off beet stems and cut beets crosswise into 1/4-inch-thick slices.
4. Divide salad greens among 4 side plates, drizzle with mustard vinaigrette, and top each serving with beets.

Mustard Vinaigrette

Large lemon, or 1/4 cup white wine vinegar
Large clove garlic
Large egg
2 tablespoons Dijon mustard
3/4 cup olive oil or vegetable oil
1/2 teaspoon salt
Freshly ground pepper

1. Squeeze enough lemon juice to measure 1/4 cup. Peel garlic.
2. Place all ingredients in food processor fitted with steel blade or in blender and process 1 minute.
3. Just before using, process vinaigrette briefly to recombine.

ADDED TOUCH

Single layers of this cake may be split and served with whipped cream and strawberry or raspberry sauce.

Tennessee Black Cake

Cake:
2 sticks unsalted butter, approximately
2 teaspoons cocoa powder
4 squares unsweetened chocolate
   (4 ounces)
2 1/2 cups all-purpose flour
1/4 teaspoon salt
2 cups granulated sugar
2 teaspoons baking soda
4 large eggs

1 cup buttermilk
2 teaspoons vanilla extract

Frosting:
1 stick unsalted butter
4 squares unsweetened chocolate
   (4 ounces)
1/2 cup evaporated milk
1-pound box confectioners' sugar
1 teaspoon vanilla extract
Salt

Optional garnishes:
1 cup heavy cream
1 pint strawberries
1 tablespoon sugar

1. To make cake: Preheat oven to 350 degrees and place rack in middle of oven. Lightly grease two 8 1/2-inch-round baking pans and dust each with 1 teaspoon cocoa powder. Cut 2 sticks butter into 8 pieces each.
2. Combine 4 squares chocolate and butter in top of double boiler set over, not in, barely simmering water and stir occasionally until melted, 1 to 2 minutes. Remove chocolate from heat and set aside to cool.
3. Sift flour, salt, granulated sugar, and baking soda into medium-size bowl. Break eggs into large bowl and beat with buttermilk and 2 teaspoons vanilla.
4. Gradually add flour mixture to egg mixture, stirring until well blended. Slowly pour in melted chocolate, stirring until smooth. Divide batter between pans.
5. Place pans in oven and bake 25 to 30 minutes, or until toothpick inserted in center of cake layers comes out clean. Be careful not to overbake.
6. Cool cake in pans on wire racks, about 10 minutes. Layers may sink slightly in center.
7. Remove layers from pans, place on racks, and allow to cool completely before frosting.
8. To make frosting: Cut 1 stick butter into 8 pieces. Place chocolate and butter in top of double boiler set over, not in, barely simmering water and stir occasionally until melted, 1 to 2 minutes. Remove chocolate from heat and set aside to cool.
9. Combine milk, confectioners' sugar, vanilla extract, and a pinch of salt in medium-size bowl, and stir until blended. Stir in cooled chocolate and beat mixture vigorously with wooden spoon until frosting thickens to spreading consistency.
10. If using heavy cream for garnish, place bowl and beaters in refrigerator to chill.
11. With icing spatula or table knife, generously frost one layer of cake. Top with second layer and frost top and sides of cake.
12. Wash strawberries, if using, hull, and dry with paper towels. Halve strawberries and arrange on top of cake.
13. Pour heavy cream into chilled bowl, add 1 tablespoon sugar, and with electric beater at high speed, beat until cream holds soft shape, about 1 to 2 minutes. Spoon whipped cream into small bowl, and serve with cake.

Corn Chowder
Sauté of Smithfield Ham and Vegetables
Cheddar Cheese Biscuits

Serve corn chowder in soup bowls or mugs, followed by sautéed ham and vegetables and a basket of cheese biscuits.

For the corn chowder in this traditional southern meal, select ears with clean green husks and golden-brown silk. Pull back the husks and check the kernels; they should be plump, not dry looking. Cook fresh corn as soon as possible after buying it.

For the main course, Smithfield ham is sautéed with jícama and other vegetables. Genuine Smithfield ham is often hard to obtain, but you can substitute another smoked country ham or, for a milder, less-salty flavor, use prosciutto (stir fry prosciutto quickly or it will toughen).

Although the tropical root vegetable jícama looks similar to a brown-skinned turnip, its crisp white flesh tastes like a combination of apple and water chestnut. Jícama is available in well-stocked supermarkets, either whole or in pieces, and can be refrigerated for a week or two. (Store small cut pieces in water to preserve their crispness and prevent drying.) You may substitute turnips for jícama.

WHAT TO DRINK

A very crisp, very dry white California Sauvignon Blanc would be ideal with these dishes. Or try a Sancerre or Pouilly-Fumé.

33

SHOPPING LIST AND STAPLES

½- to ¾-pound slice Smithfield ham, smoked country ham, or prosciutto
2½ pounds jícama, or 2½ pounds turnips
3 medium-size zucchini (about 1½ pounds total weight)
3 or 4 ears fresh corn or two 12-ounce cans corn kernels
Small bunch celery
Large red bell pepper
Small onion
Small bunch parsley for garnish (optional)
Large lemon
2 cups milk, plus 1 or 2 tablespoons (optional)
½ pint heavy cream
½ pint light cream
1 stick unsalted butter plus 7 tablespoons salted
2 ounces Cheddar cheese
1 cup plus 2 tablespoons all-purpose flour, approximately
½ teaspoon sugar (optional)
1½ teaspoons baking powder
Salt
Freshly ground pepper

UTENSILS

Food processor or blender
Large wok or sauté pan
Small skillet or butter warmer
Large heavy-gauge saucepan with cover
Small heavy-gauge saucepan
Medium-size bowl
15 x 10-inch baking sheet
Wire rack
Measuring cups and spoons
1½-inch biscuit cutter
Chef's knife
Paring knife
2 wooden spoons or wok spatulas
Spatula
Metal tongs
Vegetable peeler
Whisk
Grater
Juicer
Cutting board or pastry board

START-TO-FINISH STEPS

1. Follow biscuits recipe step 1.
2. Follow sauté recipe steps 1 through 4.
3. Follow chowder recipe steps 1 through 6.
4. Follow biscuits recipe steps 2 through 4, and chowder recipe step 7.
5. Follow biscuits recipe steps 5 and 6, and chowder recipe steps 8 and 9.
6. Follow biscuits recipe step 7.
7. Follow sauté recipe steps 5 through 7, biscuits recipe step 8, chowder recipe step 10, and serve.

RECIPES

Corn Chowder

3 or 4 ears fresh corn or two 12-ounce cans corn kernels
Small onion
1 stalk celery
4 tablespoons salted butter
½ teaspoon sugar (optional)
Small bunch parsley for garnish (optional)
2 tablespoons all-purpose flour
1 cup light cream
2 cups milk
Salt
Freshly ground pepper

1. Remove husks and silk from corn. With chef's knife, trim off stem end. Holding 1 ear of corn upright, press base against table and, with chef's knife, cut off kernels by

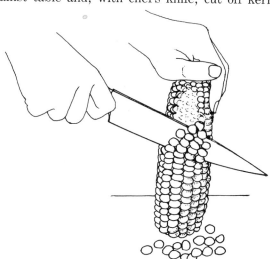

pressing blade against cob and slicing downward (see illustration). Turn corn and repeat process until all kernels are removed. Repeat process for remaining ears.

2. Peel onion and mince enough to measure ½ cup. Trim celery and mince enough to measure ¼ cup.

3. In large heavy-gauge saucepan, melt butter over medium heat until bubbly. Add onion, celery, and corn, and cook, stirring constantly with wooden spoon, until onion is soft and translucent, about 5 minutes.

4. Taste corn; if it does not seem naturally sweet, add sugar. Lower heat, cover pan, and cook another 5 minutes, or until onion and celery are very soft and corn is tender.

5. Meanwhile, if using parsley for garnish, rinse and dry with paper towels. Set aside 4 sprigs, reserving remainder for another use.

6. Add flour to corn mixture, reduce heat to medium-low, and cook, stirring, 1 or 2 minutes. Add cream and milk all at once and continue to cook, stirring occasionally, until simmering, about 7 minutes.

7. Stir in salt and pepper to taste. Set soup aside to cool slightly before puréeing.

8. Place soup in food processor fitted with steel blade or in blender and pulse once or twice to purée coarsely. Return soup to saucepan; set aside.

9. Place soup bowls under hot running water. Gently reheat soup over low heat.

10. Dry bowls, divide soup among them, and, if desired, garnish each with a parsley sprig.

Sauté of Smithfield Ham and Vegetables

Large red bell pepper
3 medium-size zucchini (about 1½ pounds total weight)
2½ pounds jícama, or 2½ pounds turnips
½- to ¾-pound slice Smithfield ham, smoked country
   ham, or prosciutto
Large lemon
1 stick unsalted butter
Freshly ground pepper

1. Rinse red bell pepper and zucchini; dry with paper towels. Halve, core, and seed pepper; trim zucchini. Peel jícama. Cut vegetables into ¼-inch-thick julienne.

2. Trim fat from ham and discard. Cut enough ham into ¼-inch-thick julienne to measure 2 cups; reserve remainder for another use.

3. Squeeze lemon and place juice in small heavy-gauge saucepan. Bring to a boil over medium heat, and reduce to

about 1 tablespoon, 2 to 3 minutes. Remove pan from heat and allow to cool slightly.

4. Cut 6 tablespoons butter into small pieces. Add to lemon juice, piece by piece, beating after each addition until incorporated. It may be necessary to warm mixture briefly, over very low heat, but butter must soften, not melt, in juice. When thoroughly combined, set aside.

5. Melt remaining 2 tablespoons butter in large wok or sauté pan over medium heat. When butter foams, add red pepper, zucchini, jícama, and ham, and sauté, stirring and tossing with wooden spoons, until vegetables are well coated with butter and starting to cook. Add 2 tablespoons water and continue to sauté, stirring and tossing until vegetables are crisp-tender, about 4 minutes.

6. If more than 2 or 3 tablespoons liquid remain in pan after vegetables are done, pour off.

7. Remove pan from heat, add lemon butter, and toss vegetables until evenly coated. Add pepper to taste and transfer to serving platter.

Cheddar Cheese Biscuits

3 tablespoons salted butter
2 ounces Cheddar cheese
1 cup all-purpose flour, approximately
1½ teaspoons baking powder
½ teaspoon salt
½ cup heavy cream
1 or 2 tablespoons milk (optional)

1. Preheat oven to 425 degrees.

2. Melt butter over low heat in small skillet or butter warmer and set aside.

3. Grate enough cheese to measure about ½ cup.

4. Combine grated cheese, 1 cup flour, baking powder, and salt in medium-size bowl. Stir in cream with fork, mixing just until moistened. Add 1 or 2 tablespoons milk to dough if too crumbly.

5. On lightly floured surface, knead dough 8 to 10 times. With fingers, press out to a scant ½-inch thickness. Cut dough into 1½-inch rounds with biscuit cutter.

6. With tongs, dip biscuits in melted butter to coat and place on ungreased baking sheet. Transfer to oven and bake 12 to 15 minutes, or until biscuits are golden.

7. Remove baking sheet from oven and place on wire rack to cool slightly.

8. With spatula, transfer biscuits from baking sheet to napkin-lined basket.

David Kimmel
and Steven Petusevsky

MENU 1 (Right)
Medallions of Pork with Apple and Onion Rings
Steamed New Potatoes and Cherry Tomatoes
in Dill Butter
Bavarian Spinach Salad

MENU 2
German-style Roast Pork
Potato and Onion Casserole
Red Cabbage and Apple Sauté

MENU 3
Hazelnut-Mustard Pork Chops
Bowtie Noodles with Poppy Seed Butter
Marinated Pepper, Fennel, and Scallion Salad

All three of these menus use ingredients popular in Germany, a country where fresh pork and smoked pork products are staples and where there is a butcher shop on nearly every corner. David Kimmel and Steven Petusevsky, both from families with Eastern European roots, have taken authentic regional German recipes and lightened and modernized them to suit American tastes. "There is a new kind of cooking coming out of Germany," says David Kimmel. "What used to be heavy, uninspired food is now much more exciting. Our menus reflect this new German cuisine."

In Menu 1, the cooks first sear and then bake pork medallions—considered the filet mignon of the pig because they are so lean and tender—and top them with a mixture of browned onions, apple slices, apple butter, and Calvados. With the pork, they serve new potatoes and cherry tomatoes with dill-seasoned sweet butter and a crisp spinach salad.

Caraway seeds are finely ground with marjoram, lemon zest and minced garlic to flavor the roast pork loin in Menu 2. As a side dish, the cooks offer a potato and onion casserole in which the natural starch of the potatoes thickens the onion juices to form a creamy sauce. Sautéed red cabbage and apples, a popular German combination, accompany the pork and potatoes.

In Menu 3, pork chops bake in a hazelnut-mustard-garlic crust that retains the meat's natural juices. Bowtie noodles coated with poppy seed butter and a salad of red bell peppers and fennel accompany the main course.

Browned pork medallions crowned with sliced apple rings and caramelized onions are served with new potatoes and cherry tomatoes coated in dill butter. A glass bowl shows off the colorful mixed salad tossed with walnut oil vinaigrette.

Medallions of Pork with Apple and Onion Rings
Steamed New Potatoes and Cherry Tomatoes in Dill Butter
Bavarian Spinach Salad

Ask your butcher for the small ends trimmed from the pork tenderloins, which you can use for another meal. They are delicious diced and stir fried with garlic, onions, and vegetables.

New red- or white-skinned potatoes, with their firm waxy texture, will not crumble when steamed. Although these potatoes require no peeling, their appearance is enhanced by removing a thin strip of skin from around the circumference. Select firm potatoes of similar size that do not have sprouts and are free of blemishes or green patches. Never store potatoes in the refrigerator; their starch will turn to sugar, making them too sweet.

Bavaria Blue, a creamy blue-veined German cheese, is sold at most cheese shops and well-stocked supermarkets. Check for even distribution of veins—a sign of good flavor. Avoid any cheese that looks dry because it will break into pieces before you can dice it.

WHAT TO DRINK

A soft, floral *Kabinett*-class Riesling from Piesport, Bernkastel, or Wehlen in the Mosel region would suit this German menu. Or try a similar wine from Johannisberg, Eltville, or Rüdesheim in the Rheingau region.

SHOPPING LIST AND STAPLES

2 tenderloins of pork (1 to 1¼ pounds total weight), each
  cut and pounded into four ½-inch-thick medallions
2 pounds small new potatoes
2 pounds spinach
1 pint cherry tomatoes
1 bunch red radishes
Large onion
Small bunch dill
Small lemon plus additional lemon, if not using white
  wine vinegar
Large tart apple, preferably Granny Smith
6 tablespoons unsalted butter
6 ounces blue cheese, preferably Bavaria
11-ounce jar apple butter
½ cup walnut or hazelnut oil, or ¼ cup nut oil plus ¼ cup
  peanut or olive oil
2 tablespoons peanut oil
2 tablespoons white wine vinegar or lemon juice
4-ounce can walnut pieces
½ teaspoon dry mustard
Salt

Freshly ground black pepper
Freshly ground white pepper
¼ cup Calvados or other apple brandy
3 tablespoons dry white wine

UTENSILS

Large heavy-gauge sauté pan or skillet
Large saucepan with cover
Small saucepan
Vegetable steamer
Large ovenproof baking dish
Large flat platter
Large bowl
2 small bowls
Salad spinner (optional)
Measuring cups and spoons
Chef's knife
Paring knife
2 wooden spoons
Spatula
Small whisk
Vegetable brush
Metal tongs
Pastry brush

START-TO-FINISH STEPS

Thirty minutes ahead: Follow salad recipe step 1.

1. Follow salad recipe steps 2 and 3.
2. Follow medallions recipe steps 1 through 7.
3. Follow potatoes recipe steps 1 through 3.
4. Follow medallions recipe steps 8 and 9.
5. Follow salad recipe steps 4 and 5.
6. Follow potatoes recipe steps 4 through 6.
7. Follow medallions recipe step 10, potatoes recipe step 7, and serve with salad.

RECIPES

Medallions of Pork with Apple and Onion Rings

Large onion
Small lemon
2 tenderloins of pork (1 to 1¼ pounds total weight), each
  cut and pounded into four ½-inch-thick medallions
Salt and freshly ground white pepper

Cutting lengthwise, remove thin strip of skin from each potato.

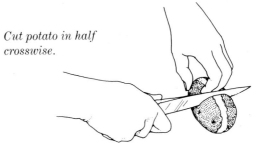

Cut potato in half crosswise.

¼ cup Calvados or other apple brandy
2 tablespoons peanut oil
2 tablespoons unsalted butter
½ cup apple butter
3 tablespoons dry white wine
Large tart apple, preferably Granny Smith

1. Preheat oven to 475 degrees.
2. Peel onion and cut crosswise into ¼-inch-thick slices; separate into rings and set aside. Squeeze lemon and set juice aside in small bowl.
3. Season both sides of medallions with salt and pepper to taste and arrange in a single layer on platter. Sprinkle each medallion with 1 teaspoon Calvados.
4. In large heavy-gauge sauté pan or skillet, heat 1 tablespoon oil and 1 tablespoon butter over medium-high heat, until almost smoking. Add 4 medallions and sear quickly, turning once, 1 or 2 minutes per side. Using metal tongs, transfer medallions to large ovenproof baking dish, arranging in a single layer. Without adding more fat to pan, repeat process for remaining medallions.
5. Return sauté pan to medium-high heat, add remaining oil and butter, and heat until almost smoking. Add onions and cook, without turning, 1 or 2 minutes. Then, turn onions and sauté until golden brown, another 1 or 2 minutes, stirring only if they begin to stick to pan.
6. Meanwhile, combine apple butter, wine, and lemon juice in small bowl, and stir until blended. Set aside.
7. When onions are browned, sprinkle with remaining Calvados, add 1 tablespoon apple butter mixture, and stir to blend. Remove pan from heat.
8. Peel and core apple. Cut apple crosswise into eight ¼-inch-thick rings.
9. Brush medallions with remaining apple butter mixture. Top each with 1 apple ring and 1½ tablespoons onions. Place baking dish in oven 8 to 10 minutes, or until medallions are heated through.
10. Remove baking dish from oven and, using spatula, carefully transfer 2 medallions to each dinner plate.

Steamed New Potatoes and Cherry Tomatoes in Dill Butter

2 pounds small new potatoes
1 pint cherry tomatoes
Small bunch dill
4 tablespoons unsalted butter
Salt and freshly ground white pepper

1. Scrub potatoes and dry with paper towels. With paring knife, remove ½-inch strip of skin from circumference of each. Cut potatoes in half across peeled area (see illustration above).
2. In large saucepan fitted with vegetable steamer, bring about 2 inches water to a boil over high heat; steamer should rest above water.
3. Place potatoes in steamer, cover tightly, and steam 12 to 15 minutes, or until potatoes are tender when pierced with tip of knife.
4. Meanwhile, rinse and dry cherry tomatoes; set aside. Wash dill and dry with paper towels; chop enough to measure 2 tablespoons and set aside. Reserve remaining dill for another use.
5. About 5 minutes before potatoes are done, add tomatoes to steamer.
6. In small saucepan, melt butter over low heat. Remove from heat, add dill, salt and pepper to taste, and stir.
7. Transfer potatoes and tomatoes to large bowl. Add dill butter and stir gently with wooden spoon to coat potatoes and tomatoes. Divide among 4 dinner plates.

Bavarian Spinach Salad

6 ounces blue cheese, preferably Bavaria
2 pounds spinach
1 cup red radishes
¾ cup walnut pieces
½ cup walnut or hazelnut oil, or ¼ cup nut oil plus ¼ cup peanut or olive oil
2 tablespoons white wine vinegar or lemon juice
½ teaspoon dry mustard
Salt and freshly ground black pepper

1. Place blue cheese in freezer to chill for at least 30 minutes.
2. Wash spinach thoroughly and remove stems. Dry spinach in salad spinner or with paper towels and refrigerate.
3. Wash, trim, and dry radishes; refrigerate until needed.
4. Remove cheese from freezer. With paring knife, trim rind and cut cheese into ½-inch dice. Cut radishes into thin slices. In large salad bowl, combine spinach, cheese, radishes, and walnuts.
5. In small bowl, combine oil, vinegar or lemon juice, mustard, and salt and pepper to taste, and whisk until thoroughly blended. Pour dressing over salad and toss well. Cover bowl with plastic wrap and refrigerate until ready to serve.

German-style Roast Pork
Potato and Onion Casserole
Red Cabbage and Apple Sauté

Full-bodied dark beer, garlic, and caraway seeds flavor the pork as it roasts. Grinding the caraway seeds releases their full flavor. If you don't have a mortar and pestle, use the back of a wooden spoon. Rather than traditionally slow-braising the accompanying apples and cabbage, sauté them quickly for a crisper texture. When shopping, select a solid head of cabbage that seems heavy for its size and shows no signs of discoloration. Store the unwashed head of cabbage in a plastic bag in the refrigerator for up to a week.

Pale dinnerware dramatizes the contrasting colors and textures of sliced pork tenderloin, sautéed red cabbage and apples, and potato and onion casserole. Spoon the beer-enriched sauce over each portion of pork before serving.

WHAT TO DRINK

This hearty, flavorful meal could be accompanied either by the same dark beer used in the pork sauce or by a top-quality Alsatian Gewürztraminer or Riesling.

SHOPPING LIST AND STAPLES

1¾-pound boneless center loin pork roast, cut in half
4 medium-size potatoes (about 1½ pounds total weight)
Small head red cabbage
Small bunch celery
Medium-size onion plus 1 small

Medium-size carrot
Small bunch watercress for garnish (optional)
Small bunch fresh marjoram, or ½ teaspoon dried
2 large cloves garlic
Medium-size lemon
2 small tart apples, preferably Granny Smith
2 cups chicken stock, preferably homemade (see page 13), or canned
8½-ounce carton cranberry juice, or 8-ounce jar cranberry sauce (optional)
8-ounce jar applesauce (optional)
3 tablespoons unsalted butter, approximately
1½ tablespoons peanut oil
1 tablespoon red wine vinegar
2½ tablespoons sugar

1 tablespoon cornstarch
1 bay leaf
1 tablespoon caraway seeds
Salt
Freshly ground black pepper
Freshly ground white pepper
12-ounce bottle dark beer

UTENSILS

Large heavy-gauge sauté pan or saucepan
10 x 14-inch roasting pan
2- or 3-inch-deep flameproof casserole or baking dish
Platter
Large stainless steel or glass bowl

2 small bowls (plus 1 additional if not using mortar and
  pestle)
Colander
Coarse strainer
Measuring cups and spoons
Chef's knife
Paring knife
2 wooden spoons
Mortar and pestle (optional)
Spatula
Meat thermometer
Vegetable peeler
Zester (optional)

START-TO-FINISH STEPS

1. Follow pork recipe steps 1 through 5.
2. Follow casserole recipe steps 1 through 4.
3. Follow cabbage recipe step 1.
4. Follow pork recipe step 6 and casserole recipe step 5.
5. Follow cabbage recipe steps 2 through 6.
6. Follow pork recipe step 7 and casserole recipe step 6.
7. Follow pork recipe step 8 and casserole recipe step 7.
8. Follow pork recipe steps 9 and 10, and casserole recipe
step 8.
9. Follow pork recipe steps 11 and 12, casserole recipe step
9, and serve with cabbage.

RECIPES

German-style Roast Pork

2 large cloves garlic
Medium-size lemon
Small bunch fresh marjoram or ½ teaspoon dried
1 tablespoon caraway seeds
Salt and freshly ground black pepper
1¾-pound boneless center loin pork roast, cut in half
Medium-size carrot
Small onion
1 stalk celery
1 cup dark beer
¾ cup chicken stock
1 bay leaf
1 tablespoon cornstarch

1. Preheat oven to 475 degrees.
2. Peel garlic and mince enough to measure 2 tablespoons.

Wash and dry lemon; remove zest and mince, reserving
fruit for another use. If using fresh marjoram, rinse and
dry with paper towels; chop coarsely.
3. Combine garlic, lemon zest, marjoram, caraway seeds,
and salt and pepper to taste in mortar or small bowl, and
grind finely with pestle or back of wooden spoon. Rub
spice mixture into each tenderloin.
4. With vegetable peeler, scrape carrot, then dice enough
to measure about ½ cup. Peel and halve onion, reserving
one half for another use. Dice enough of remaining half to
measure ¼ cup. Wash celery, dry, and dice enough to
measure ½ cup.
5. Scatter carrot, onion, and celery over bottom of lightly
oiled roasting pan. Top with pork and drizzle with 2 tablespoons dark beer. Place pork in oven and roast 20 minutes.
6. After 20 minutes, check pork to ensure even browning
and lower oven temperature to 400 degrees. If most of pan
liquid has evaporated, add ¼ cup chicken stock to moisten
vegetables. Continue roasting pork another 30 minutes.
7. When meat thermometer registers 170 degrees, pierce
pork with knife tip to test for desired degree of doneness:
Juices should run clear. Transfer pork to platter and cover
loosely with foil to keep warm.
8. Place roasting pan, with vegetables and pan drippings,
on stove over medium-high heat. Add remaining beer and
bay leaf, and scrape up brown bits clinging to bottom of
pan with spatula or wooden spoon. Reduce liquid by about
one half, 5 to 7 minutes.
9. Add remaining chicken stock and bring mixture to a
boil. Reduce heat to medium and simmer 5 minutes.
10. In small bowl, blend cornstarch with 2 tablespoons
water.
11. While stirring constantly, gradually add cornstarch to
sauce. Pour sauce through coarse strainer set over small
bowl, pressing with back of spoon to extrude as much
liquid as possible. Discard solids left in strainer. Stir in
salt and pepper to taste.
12. Cut each pork loin into 6 slices and divide among
dinner plates. Drizzle with sauce and serve.

Potato and Onion Casserole

4 sprigs watercress for garnish (optional)
4 medium-size potatoes (about 1½ pounds total weight)
Medium-size onion
2 tablespoons unsalted butter, approximately
Salt and freshly ground white pepper
1¼ cups chicken stock, approximately

1. Grease flameproof baking dish and set aside. If using watercress for garnish, wash 4 sprigs and dry, reserving remainder for another use.
2. Wash potatoes, drain in colander, and cut crosswise into ⅛-inch-thick slices. Peel onion and cut crosswise into ⅛-inch-thick slices.
3. Cut 2 tablespoons butter into small pieces.
4. In greased baking dish, alternate layers of potato and onion slices, dotting each layer with butter and sprinkling with salt and pepper. Pour chicken stock over top layer and cover dish with foil.
5. Place casserole on lower rack in 400-degree oven and bake 30 minutes.
6. Remove foil and bake casserole another 10 minutes, or until potatoes are tender when pierced with tip of knife.
7. Remove casserole from oven, cover loosely with foil, and set aside. Turn on broiler.
8. Place baking dish under broiler about 4 inches from heat for 5 minutes, or until top layer of casserole is lightly browned.
9. Divide potatoes and onions among 4 dinner plates, and garnish with watercress, if desired.

Red Cabbage and Apple Sauté

Small head red cabbage
2 small tart apples, preferably Granny Smith
1½ tablespoons peanut oil
1 tablespoon unsalted butter
2½ tablespoons sugar
1 tablespoon red wine vinegar
1½ tablespoons cranberry juice, or 1 tablespoon cranberry sauce (optional)
Salt and freshly ground black pepper
2 tablespoons applesauce (optional)

1. Wash cabbage and apples, and dry with paper towels. Quarter cabbage, core, and cut quarters crosswise into ¼-inch-thick slices; set aside in large stainless-steel or glass bowl.
2. In large heavy-gauge sauté pan or saucepan, heat oil and butter over medium-high heat. Add cabbage and sauté 3 or 4 minutes, stirring, or until slices are glossy and have just begun to soften.
3. While cabbage is cooking, quarter and core apples; cut into ¼-inch-thick slices.
4. Add apples and sugar to cabbage and sauté another 1 or 2 minutes.

5. Add vinegar, cranberry juice or sauce, if using, and salt and pepper to taste. Cook mixture, stirring frequently, 2 to 3 minutes, until cabbage is crisp-tender and most of the liquid has evaporated.
6. Remove pan from heat and stir in applesauce, if using. Cover pan and set on back of stove to keep warm.

ADDED TOUCH

Use only very soft avocados in this rich chilled dessert. To get the best consistency, make the dessert before dinner and freeze it for about an hour and a half. You can also make it and freeze it a day ahead. Either way, be sure to remove it about 15 minutes before serving to soften.

Fluffy Avocado Cream

1 cup vanilla ice cream
Small lime
¼ cup heavy cream
2 very ripe avocados
¼ cup confectioners' sugar
2 tablespoons kirschwasser or other cherry-flavored brandy
2 unhulled strawberries for garnish (optional)

1. Set out 1 cup vanilla ice cream at room temperature to soften. Place food processor bowl, if using, electric mixer beaters, and small mixing bowl in freezer for 5 minutes to chill.
2. Cut lime in half, reserving one half for another use; squeeze remaining half to measure 1 teaspoon juice.
3. Remove bowl and beaters from freezer and, with electric mixer set at high speed, whip heavy cream until it holds a soft shape. Set whipped cream aside.
4. Halve avocados, remove pits, and scoop flesh into chilled bowl of food processor fitted with steel blade. Add lime juice, confectioners' sugar, and kirschwasser, and purée. Or, combine ingredients in medium-size bowl and mash to a fine purée with wooden spoon.
5. Spoon avocado cream into plastic container, cover tightly, and place in freezer until ready to serve. At least an hour and a half ahead, place 4 wine or parfait glasses in refrigerator to chill.
6. About 15 minutes before serving, divide avocado cream among 4 glasses and allow to soften at room temperature. If using strawberries, wash, dry, cut in half, and set aside.
7. Just before serving, garnish each dessert with half a strawberry.

Hazelnut-Mustard Pork Chops
Bowtie Noodles with Poppy Seed Butter
Marinated Pepper, Fennel, and Scallion Salad

Hazelnut-encrusted pork chops are garnished with sprigs of parsley and served with bowtie noodles tossed in poppy seed butter. A salad of marinated peppers, scallions, and fennel is an appealing and refreshing accompaniment to the entrée.

The delicate flavor of fresh fennel in the salad is boosted by the addition of Pernod, a French licorice-flavored aperitif with a light yellow-green color. You can substitute ouzo or anisette for Pernod.

WHAT TO DRINK

Either dark beer or a full-bodied white wine would go well here. If you choose wine, try a California Chardonnay or Chablis, which you can also use in preparing the pork chops.

SHOPPING LIST AND STAPLES

Eight ½-inch-thick loin pork chops (about 2½ pounds total weight)
2 medium-size fennel bulbs
Medium-size green bell pepper
Medium-size red bell pepper
1 bunch scallions
Medium-size clove garlic
Small bunch parsley
Large lemon
4 tablespoons unsalted butter, plus 1½ tablespoons (optional)
½ cup olive oil
¼ cup peanut or olive oil, approximately
5 tablespoons plus 1 teaspoon coarse-grain mustard, preferably Pommery
¼ cup Dijon mustard
¾ pound bowtie-shaped egg noodles
1 slice stale bread
½ pound hazelnuts in the shell, or ¼ pound shelled pecans
2¾-ounce jar poppy seeds
½ teaspoon ground nutmeg
Salt
Freshly ground black pepper
Freshly ground white pepper
¼ cup dry white wine, preferably Chablis
1 to 3 teaspoons Pernod

UTENSILS

Food processor or blender
2 large heavy-gauge sauté pans or skillets
Small heavy-gauge skillet
Large saucepan
Small saucepan

17 x 11-inch baking pan
9-inch pie pan
2 medium-size bowls, 1 shallow
Small bowl
Colander
Measuring cups and spoons
Chef's knife
Paring knife
Wooden spoon
Metal tongs

START-TO-FINISH STEPS

Thirty minutes ahead: Set out 4 tablespoons unsalted butter to soften for noodles recipe.

1. Follow pork chops recipe steps 1 through 6.
2. Follow noodles recipe steps 1 through 4.
3. Follow pork chops recipe steps 7 through 10.
4. Follow noodles recipe step 5 and salad recipe steps 1 and 2.
5. Follow noodles recipe steps 6 and 7, pork chops recipe step 11, and serve with salad.

RECIPES

Hazelnut-Mustard Pork Chops

5 tablespoons plus 1 teaspoon coarse-grain mustard, preferably Pommery
¼ cup Dijon mustard
¼ cup dry white wine, preferably Chablis
½ pound hazelnuts in the shell, or 1 cup shelled pecans
1 slice stale bread
Medium-size clove garlic
Small bunch parsley
1½ tablespoons unsalted butter (optional)
¼ cup peanut or olive oil, approximately
Eight ½-inch-thick loin pork chops (about 2½ pounds total weight)
Freshly ground black pepper

1. Preheat oven to 375 degrees.
2. In shallow medium-size bowl, combine coarse-grain and Dijon mustards with wine and set aside.
3. Shell enough hazelnuts to measure 1 cup and chop coarsely in food processor or blender. Transfer to pie pan.
4. Break bread into pieces, place in food processor or blender, and process.
5. Peel garlic and mince enough to measure 1½ teaspoons. Wash parsley and dry with paper towels. Set aside 8 sprigs for garnish, if desired, and chop enough of remainder to measure 2 to 3 tablespoons.
6. Add garlic, 2 to 3 tablespoons chopped parsley, and bread crumbs to ground nuts in pie pan and stir with fork to combine; set aside.
7. If using butter, melt in small saucepan over medium heat, about 30 seconds, and set aside.
8. Heat 1½ to 2 tablespoons oil in each of 2 large heavy-gauge sauté pans or skillets over medium-high heat. Score

fat on chops to prevent meat from curling. Sprinkle chops with freshly ground pepper to taste, divide them between pans, and sear about 1 to 2 minutes per side.
9. With tongs, dip chops one by one into mustard-wine mixture, coating both sides. Then place each chop in hazelnut-crumb mixture to coat, using palm of your hand to press crumbs into chops to make them adhere.
10. Place coated chops in large baking pan, drizzle with melted butter, if using, and bake 20 minutes, or until crust forms on top and chops are cooked through but still juicy.
11. Transfer chops to platter and garnish with parsley sprigs, if desired.

Bowtie Noodles with Poppy Seed Butter

Salt
1½ tablespoons poppy seeds
4 tablespoons unsalted butter, at room temperature
½ teaspoon ground nutmeg
¾ pound bowtie-shaped egg noodles
Freshly ground black pepper

1. In large saucepan, bring 3 quarts water and 1 tablespoon salt to a rolling boil over medium-high heat.
2. Meanwhile, toast poppy seeds in small dry heavy-gauge skillet over medium heat, shaking skillet frequently until seeds begin to pop and become fragrant, about 5 minutes. Transfer seeds to small plate and set aside to cool.
3. In small bowl, blend butter, nutmeg, and poppy seeds with wooden spoon; set aside.
4. Add noodles to boiling water and cook 10 to 12 minutes, or until *al dente*.
5. Turn noodles into colander to drain; dry saucepan.
6. Heat 2 tablespoons of poppy seed butter in same saucepan over medium-high heat. Add noodles, salt and pepper to taste, and stir until noodles are heated through.
7. Turn noodles into bowl and serve immediately.

Marinated Pepper, Fennel, and Scallion Salad

2 medium-size fennel bulbs
Medium-size green bell pepper
Medium-size red bell pepper
6 scallions
2 tablespoons lemon juice
½ cup olive oil
1 to 3 teaspoons Pernod
Salt and freshly ground white pepper

1. Wash and dry fennel, bell peppers, and scallions. Cut fennel bulbs in half lengthwise; reserve half of 1 bulb for another use. Remove outer leaves and center cores of remaining fennel. Halve bell peppers, core, and remove seeds and membranes. Trim off roots and green parts of scallions. Cut fennel, peppers, and scallions into ¼-inch-thick julienne strips, or julienne vegetables in food processor fitted with slicing blade.
2. Place vegetables in medium-size bowl, add olive oil, and toss well. Add lemon juice, Pernod and salt and pepper to taste, and toss to combine; set aside until ready to serve.

W. Peter Prestcott

Although Peter Prestcott's menus are all influenced by foreign cuisines, they are not—as might be expected—complex. "People are overworked these days," he says, "and have little time for fancy cooking. I like to lavish care on the ingredient selection, but I always keep my recipes simple."

Each of his three menus has a distinctly different foreign flavor. In Menu 1 he features a Greek-style main course: ground pork rolled in paper-thin filo dough, a variation on a traditional lamb dish. He adds sunflower seeds to the pork filling for a nutty taste, and dried apricots (rather than the more authentic raisins) for sweetness. With the pork, he serves a yogurt and sour cream sauce and a salad of cubed feta cheese, Niçoise olives, and cherry tomatoes.

Menu 2 has a strong Italian accent. For this meal, Peter Prestcott braises pork tenderloin with fresh fennel, a popular Italian winter vegetable. He heightens the fennel's slight licorice flavor by adding anise seeds to the dish. For dessert, he presents a frozen raspberry cream.

An elegant meal reminiscent of France, Menu 3 offers an entrée of pork medallions with a thick mushroom and port sauce. The dinner begins with *croustades* (crusty slices of buttered and baked bread) topped with seasoned chicken livers.

Dried apricots and sunflower seeds enhance the natural sweetness of pork in the filling for the filo rolls. Have your guests serve themselves buffet-style, adding the tart sour cream sauce if they wish. Feta cheese, black olives, and Mediterranean herbs are included in the Greek salad.

Greek Salad
Pork in Filo with Sour Cream Sauce

Filo (meaning leaf in Greek) is a tissue-thin pastry dough that comes in sheets. Working with filo can be tricky because it dries out and crumbles when overexposed to air. However, if you work quickly and keep the pastry sheets moist, you should have no problems. Unroll the dough and lay eight sheets, unseparated, on a damp dish towel and cover them with a second damp towel. Work with one sheet of dough at a time, leaving the rest covered. The clarified butter (see page 12), which you brush on the sheets, helps to separate the layers and turns the dough a golden color as it bakes (too much butter, however, will make the pastry soggy).

Filo dough is sold in one-pound boxes in Middle Eastern markets and most supermarkets. It will keep, unopened, in the refrigerator for up to a week and in the freezer for up to a year. Thaw frozen filo overnight in the refrigerator, but never refreeze the dough or the sheets may stick together.

WHAT TO DRINK

Try a well-chilled Alsatian Gewürztraminer or a dark beer with this menu.

SHOPPING LIST AND STAPLES

1 pound ground pork
Small head Boston or Bibb lettuce
1 pint cherry tomatoes
2 bunches scallions
3 cloves garlic
Large lime
Small lemon for garnish (optional)
2 eggs
2 sticks unsalted butter
1 cup sour cream
1 cup plain yogurt
¾ pound firm feta cheese
1-pound box frozen filo dough
2 tablespoons olive oil, preferably extra-virgin
2 tablespoons vegetable oil
2 tablespoons Dijon mustard
8-ounce package dried apricots
4-ounce package sunflower seeds
¼ pound Niçoise olives, or 6½-ounce jar oil-packed small black olives
1 tablespoon ground cumin

1 tablespoon plus 1 teaspoon dried thyme
1 teaspoon dried rosemary
1 teaspoon dried tarragon
Small bay leaf for garnish (optional)
Salt and freshly ground pepper
¼ cup apricot brandy

UTENSILS

Large skillet
Small heavy-gauge saucepan or butter warmer
17 x 11-inch baking sheet
Medium-size serving bowl
Shallow serving bowl
2 medium-size bowls
Small bowl
Salad spinner (optional)
Measuring cups and spoons
Chef's knife
Paring knife
2 wooden spoons
Mortar and pestle or garlic press
Pastry brush

START-TO-FINISH STEPS

The night before: Remove 8 sheets of filo from freezer and place in refrigerator to thaw.

1. Chop scallions for pork and sauce recipes.
2. Follow pork recipe steps 1 through 3.
3. Follow salad recipe step 1.
4. Follow pork recipe step 4 and salad recipe step 2.
5. Follow pork recipe steps 5 and 6, and salad recipe step 3.
6. Follow pork recipe steps 7 through 13.
7. Follow sauce recipe steps 1 and 2.
8. Follow pork recipe step 14, sauce recipe step 3, and serve with salad.

RECIPES

Greek Salad

Small head Boston or Bibb lettuce
1 pint cherry tomatoes
¾ pound firm feta cheese
Small lemon for garnish (optional)

2 tablespoons olive oil, preferably extra-virgin
1 teaspoon dried rosemary
1 teaspoon dried tarragon
1 teaspoon dried thyme
¼ pound Niçoise olives, or 6½-ounce jar oil-packed small black olives
Small bay leaf for garnish (optional)

1. Wash lettuce and dry in salad spinner or with paper towels. Arrange leaves on bottom and sides of shallow serving bowl. Wash and dry tomatoes and remove stems. Cut feta cheese into ½-inch cubes. Rinse lemon and dry. Remove two 1½-inch-long strips of peel from lemon for garnish, if using.
2. In medium-size bowl, combine olive oil, rosemary, tarragon, and thyme. Add tomatoes and olives, and toss until evenly coated. Add cheese and toss gently to avoid breaking cubes.
3. Turn mixture into lettuce-lined bowl; arrange bay leaf and lemon strips in center of salad, if desired. Cover bowl with plastic wrap and set aside at room temperature until ready to serve.

Pork in Filo with Sour Cream Sauce

8-ounce package dried apricots
¼ cup apricot brandy
3 cloves garlic
2 sticks unsalted butter
2 tablespoons vegetable oil
2 cups chopped scallions, approximately
1 tablespoon dried thyme
¾ cup sunflower seeds
1 pound ground pork
2 eggs
1 teaspoon salt
1 teaspoon freshly ground pepper
8 sheets frozen filo dough, thawed
Sour Cream Sauce (see following recipe)

1. Coarsely chop enough apricots to measure ¾ cup and place in medium-size bowl. Add brandy, stir, and set aside.
2. Peel garlic and crush cloves in mortar with pestle or put through garlic press.
3. In large skillet, heat 6 tablespoons of the butter and the oil over medium heat. Add garlic and scallions, and sauté 5 to 7 minutes, or until scallions are softened.
4. Add thyme and sunflower seeds, and sauté 4 minutes, or until sunflower seeds are browned.
5. Preheat oven to 375 degrees.
6. Add ground pork to skillet and stir to combine. Cook filling over medium heat 10 minutes.
7. In small heavy-gauge saucepan or butter warmer, clarify 1 stick plus 2 tablespoons butter.
8. Lightly beat eggs in small bowl. Add eggs, salt, and pepper to apricots and brandy and mix well.
9. Remove skillet from heat, add egg mixture, and stir until well blended; set aside.
10. Place 1 sheet filo, with long edge toward you, on work surface and brush with 1 teaspoon clarified butter. Top

first sheet with another sheet and brush with 1 teaspoon clarified butter. Repeat process with 2 more sheets filo.
11. Leaving 1½-inch border on bottom and along 2 short sides of layered filo, spread half of pork filling along bottom edge. Fold bottom edge of dough over filling; then fold sides over filling. Roll up pork in filo to form neat 8-inch-long x 3-inch-wide roll. Transfer pork roll to large baking sheet, folded side down, and brush with butter.
12. Repeat steps 10 and 11 to form another roll.
13. Bake pork rolls in preheated oven 30 minutes, or until filo is crisp and golden brown.
14. Transfer pork rolls to cutting board, cut into 1-inch-thick slices, and serve with sour cream sauce.

Sour Cream Sauce

Large lime
1 cup sour cream
1 cup plain yogurt
2 tablespoons Dijon mustard
1 tablespoon ground cumin
½ teaspoon salt
½ teaspoon freshly ground pepper
2 tablespoons chopped scallions

1. Cut lime in half and squeeze juice. In medium-size serving dish, blend lime juice, sour cream, yogurt, mustard, cumin, salt, and pepper.
2. Cover dish with plastic wrap and set aside.
3. Just before serving, sprinkle sauce with scallions.

ADDED TOUCH

The grapes for this sweet, gingery dessert must be icy but not frozen hard to produce a sherbet-like consistency.

Iced Grapes in Honeyed Yogurt

1½ pounds seedless green grapes
1 cup golden raisins
1 cup sweet vermouth
2¾-ounce box ginger snap cookies
¼ cup honey
1 pint plain yogurt
¼ cup brown sugar

1. At least 45 minutes before serving, rinse grapes, remove stems, and dry with paper towels. Spread grapes out on baking sheet and place in freezer.
2. In small bowl, combine raisins with vermouth and set aside for 15 to 20 minutes.
3. With rolling pin, crush enough ginger snap cookies between 2 sheets of waxed paper to measure ¼ cup.
4. In another small bowl, blend honey and yogurt. Cover with plastic wrap and refrigerate. Place 4 dessert bowls in refrigerator to chill.
5. Just before serving, turn raisins into strainer to drain, discarding vermouth. Remove grapes from freezer and combine with raisins; divide among chilled dessert bowls. Spoon honeyed yogurt over fruit and sprinkle with cookie crumbs and brown sugar.

Braised Pork with Fennel and Onion
Snow Peas with Pecans
Raspberry Snow

Use your best dinnerware for this meal of pork with fennel and onion, snow peas with pecans, and raspberry snow.

Braising is a cooking technique usually employed to tenderize tough cuts of meat and fibrous vegetables. Although the tenderloin is the most tender cut of pork, the cook braises it here for 20 minutes to bring out the full character and flavor of the meat. With the pork, he cooks fennel, a refreshing vegetable available in late fall and winter at Italian markets, greengrocers, and well-stocked supermarkets. Fennel may be sold with or without its white ribs and feathery leaves. For this recipe, use the inner ribs.

The dessert recipe calls for frozen raspberries in syrup; you may use fresh berries instead, but add extra sugar to compensate for the lack of syrup. Raspberry snow can be made up to four hours before serving. If kept longer, the egg whites may begin to break down.

WHAT TO DRINK

Complement the main course with a crisp white California Chardonnay or a dry Chenin Blanc.

SHOPPING LIST AND STAPLES

2 pounds tenderloin of pork
¼ pound lean bacon
1½ pounds snow peas
3 fennel bulbs, or 1 bunch celery (about 1½ pounds total weight)
Large onion (about 1 pound)
Large bunch dill
Small lemon
3 eggs
2 tablespoons unsalted butter
½ pint heavy cream
10-ounce package frozen raspberries in syrup
10-ounce bottle apple juice
1 cup chicken stock, preferably homemade (see page 13), or canned
1 tablespoon vegetable oil
2½-ounce package pecans
2 tablespoons sugar
1½ teaspoons anise seeds
Salt and freshly ground pepper

UTENSILS

Food processor or blender

Electric mixer
Large heatproof casserole or Dutch oven with cover
Medium-size skillet
Large saucepan
Vegetable steamer
Large platter
2 medium-size bowls
Colander
Sieve
Measuring cups and spoons
Chef's knife
Paring knife
2 wooden spoons
Slotted spoon
Rubber spatula
Metal tongs
Instant-reading meat thermometer
Mortar and pestle or rolling pin
Metal roasting rack

START-TO-FINISH STEPS

One hour ahead: Separate 3 eggs for raspberry snow recipe, set aside whites at room temperature and reserve yolks for another use. Remove frozen raspberries from freezer to thaw. Place heavy cream, medium-size bowl, and beaters in refrigerator to chill.

1. Follow pork recipe steps 1 through 4.
2. While onions are sautéing, follow snow peas recipe step 1.
3. Follow pork recipe steps 5 through 7.
4. While pork is braising, follow raspberry snow recipe steps 1 through 4.
5. Follow pork recipe step 8.
6. Follow snow peas recipe steps 2 and 3.
7. Follow pork recipe step 9 and serve with snow peas.
8. Follow raspberry snow recipe step 5 and serve for dessert.

RECIPES

Braised Pork with Fennel and Onion

¼ pound lean bacon
Large onion (about 1 pound)
3 fennel bulbs, or 1 bunch celery (about 1½ pounds total weight)
1½ teaspoons anise seeds

Large bunch dill
1 tablespoon vegetable oil
2 pounds tenderloin of pork
1 cup apple juice
1 cup chicken stock

1. Preheat oven to 400 degrees. Cut bacon into ¼-inch pieces. Peel onion and slice thinly. Wash and dry fennel; remove outer leaves and thinly slice inner ribs. With mortar and pestle, finely grind anise seeds. Or, place seeds between 2 sheets of waxed paper and grind with rolling pin. Wash dill, dry with paper towels, and mince enough to measure ⅓ cup, reserving 8 sprigs for garnish, if desired.
2. In large heatproof casserole or Dutch oven, heat oil over medium-high heat. Add bacon and sauté, stirring occasionally, 5 minutes, or until fat is rendered and bacon is lightly brown. With slotted spoon, transfer bacon to paper towels to drain and set aside.
3. Add pork to fat in casserole and brown over medium-high heat, turning frequently, about 5 minutes, and then transfer to metal roasting rack set on platter.
4. Reduce heat to medium. Add onions to casserole and sauté 10 minutes, or until onions are soft and translucent.
5. Remove casserole from heat and add apple juice, scraping up any bits of onion or meat that cling to bottom. Add half the fennel and stir to combine.
6. Rub pork with ground anise seeds and place on top of fennel and onion. Add remaining fennel and chicken stock, and place casserole over medium-high heat. Bring liquid to a boil, reduce heat, and simmer 3 to 4 minutes. Remove from heat.
7. Cover casserole, transfer to oven, and braise 20 minutes, or until internal temperature of pork registers 150 degrees on meat thermometer. Just before meat is done, place platter under hot running water to warm.
8. Dry platter and transfer meat and vegetables to warmed platter with slotted spoon; set aside to rest 10 minutes. Meanwhile, add minced dill to liquid in casserole and boil over high heat until reduced by half, about 10 minutes.
9. Cut pork into 8 or 12 medallions. Divide fennel and onions among 4 dinner plates and arrange 2 or 3 slices of pork on each plate. Spoon reduced pan juices over meat and vegetables and garnish with bacon and dill sprigs, if desired.

Snow Peas with Pecans

2½-ounce package pecans
Small lemon
1½ pounds snow peas
2 tablespoons unsalted butter
Salt and freshly ground pepper

1. Coarsely chop enough pecans to measure 2 tablespoons. Cut lemon in half, reserving one half for another use. Squeeze remaining half of lemon to measure 1 tablespoon juice and set aside.
2. In large saucepan fitted with vegetable steamer, bring small amount of water to a boil. Remove strings from snow peas, place in steamer and cook over boiling water 2 minutes, or until peas are bright green and crisp. Turn peas into colander, refresh under cold water, and drain.
3. In medium-size skillet, melt butter over medium heat. Add chopped pecans and sauté, stirring until browned, 1 or 2 minutes. Add snow peas and lemon juice, and cook, tossing, until coated with butter, about 1 minute. Season with salt and pepper to taste, toss again, and divide among 4 dinner plates.

Raspberry Snow

10-ounce package frozen raspberries in syrup, thawed
1 cup heavy cream, chilled
3 egg whites, at room temperature
Pinch of salt
2 tablespoons sugar

1. Place raspberries in blender or in food processor fitted with steel blade and purée. Strain purée through sieve into medium-size bowl.
2. Remove cream from refrigerator and pour into chilled medium-size bowl. Whip cream with electric mixer at high speed until stiff. With rubber spatula, gently fold whipped cream into raspberry purée.
3. Wash beaters and bowl, and dry. In same bowl, combine egg whites with pinch of salt and beat until soft peaks form. Add sugar gradually and continue beating until egg whites are stiff but not dry.
4. Fold egg whites into raspberry-cream mixture, cover with plastic wrap, and refrigerate until ready to serve.
5. Just before serving, divide raspberry snow among 4 dessert bowls or stemmed glasses.

ADDED TOUCH

Orzo is a small barley-shaped pasta popular in Greece. When grating the lemon for zest, avoid the white pith because it gives the orzo a bitter taste.

Orzo with Lemon Zest and Parsley

Salt
1 cup orzo
2 tablespoons unsalted butter, at room temperature
1 tablespoon grated lemon zest
2 tablespoons minced parsley
Freshly ground pepper

1. Preheat oven to 200 degrees.
2. In large stockpot, bring 2 quarts water and 2 tablespoons salt to a boil over high heat. Add orzo and cook 12 minutes, or until tender but still firm to the bite.
3. Turn orzo into sieve and drain thoroughly.
4. Return orzo to pot and stir in butter and lemon zest. Add 1 tablespoon parsley and salt and pepper to taste, and stir to combine.
5. Transfer orzo to ovenproof dish and keep warm in oven.
6. Just before serving, garnish orzo with remaining tablespoon parsley.

Chicken Liver Croustades
Medallions of Pork with Mushroom Sauce
Brussels Sprouts with Ginger

Serve your guests the croustades as an appetizer before the buttery Brussels sprouts and tender pork medallions.

Have your butcher cut the pork tenderloin into ¾-inch-thick medallions and tie each with string to retain its shape during cooking. For the dried mushrooms, select the variety called either *cèpes* or *porcini*, available at specialty food shops and most well-stocked supermarkets. Dried mushrooms should be stored tightly sealed in a cool spot or in your refrigerator, and used within a year.

Brussels sprouts look like miniature heads of cabbage. Good sprouts are bright green, firm, and compact. Do not trim the stems too close to the heads, or the outer leaves will fall off during cooking.

WHAT TO DRINK

A light fruity red or white wine would be a good match for these dishes. If you prefer white, choose an Italian Pinot Grigio or Chardonnay; if you want red, try a young California Zinfandel or Gamay Beaujolais.

SHOPPING LIST AND STAPLES

Eight ¾-inch-thick eye of loin pork medallions (about 2 pounds total weight)
8 chicken livers (½ to ¾ pound total weight)
2 pounds Brussels sprouts
Small head curly leaf lettuce
Small bunch parsley
4 small shallots
2-inch piece fresh ginger root
2 limes for garnish (optional)
Small lemon
1 stick plus 6 tablespoons unsalted butter
2 ounces Parmesan cheese
1 cup beef stock, preferably homemade (see page 13), or canned
¼ cup vegetable oil
1 tablespoon tarragon vinegar
4 slices home-style white bread
½ ounce dried mushrooms, such as cèpes or porcini
½ teaspoon dried tarragon
Salt and freshly ground pepper
1 cup tawny port wine

UTENSILS

Food processor (optional)
2 large skillets, 1 heavy-gauge with cover
Medium-size skillet
Large saucepan
Vegetable steamer
Small cookie sheet
Large platter
3 small bowls
Large strainer
Salad spinner (optional)
Measuring cups and spoons
Chef's knife
Paring knife
Wooden spoon
Slotted spoon
Spatula
Grater (if not using processor)

START-TO-FINISH STEPS

1. Squeeze enough lemon juice for croustades and Brussels sprouts and set aside.
2. Follow pork recipe steps 1 and 2, and croustades recipe step 1.
3. Follow pork recipe step 3 and croustades recipe steps 2 through 7.
4. Follow pork recipe steps 4 through 6 and Brussels sprouts recipe step 1.
5. Follow croustades recipe step 8 and pork recipe step 7.
6. Follow Brussels sprouts recipe step 2 and croustades recipe step 9.
7. Follow pork recipe step 8 and Brussels sprouts recipe step 3.
8. While Brussels sprouts are cooking, follow croustades recipe step 10 and serve.
9. Follow pork recipe step 9, Brussels sprouts recipe steps 4 and 5, and serve.

RECIPES

Chicken Liver Croustades

8 chicken livers (½ to ¾ pound total weight)
Small bunch parsley
4 small shallots
Small head curly leaf lettuce
4 slices home-style white bread
1 ounce Parmesan cheese
6 tablespoons unsalted butter

2 tablespoons vegetable oil
1 tablespoon lemon juice

1. Wash and dry chicken livers. Trim off any excess fat and membranes, and discard. Rinse parsley and dry with paper towels. Mince enough parsley to measure 2 tablespoons. Peel and mince shallots. Wash lettuce and dry in salad spinner or with paper towels. Divide lettuce leaves among 4 small plates. With paring knife, cut out 3-inch circle from each slice of bread. Grate enough Parmesan to measure ¼ cup.
2. In medium-size skillet, melt 3 tablespoons butter with 1 tablespoon oil over high heat until sizzling. Add chicken livers and cook about 30 seconds per side. Using slotted spoon, transfer livers to small bowl and set aside.
3. Add shallots to skillet and sauté in fat used to cook livers, 5 minutes, or until softened.
4. Add 1 tablespoon lemon juice and cook 1 minute. Scrape pan with wooden spoon, turn shallots into another small bowl, and set aside.
5. Using same skillet, melt remaining 3 tablespoons butter with remaining tablespoon oil over medium heat. Add bread and sauté, turning once, just until butter is absorbed, about 1 minute. With spatula, transfer bread rounds to small cookie sheet.
6. Cut chicken livers diagonally in half and place 4 halves on each croustade. Sprinkle 1 tablespoon Parmesan over each and set aside.
7. Preheat broiler.
8. Place croustades under broiler for 4 minutes, or until cheese melts.
9. Turn off broiler and leave oven door ajar to reduce temperature quickly.
10. Remove croustades from broiler, sprinkle each with sautéed shallots and minced parsley, and serve immediately.

Medallions of Pork with Mushroom Sauce

½ ounce dried mushrooms, such as cèpes or porcini
6 tablespoons unsalted butter
2 tablespoons vegetable oil
Eight ¾-inch-thick eye of loin pork medallions (about 2 pounds total weight)
1 cup tawny port wine
1 cup beef stock
½ teaspoon dried tarragon
2 limes for garnish, thinly sliced (optional)

1 tablespoon tarragon vinegar
Freshly ground pepper

1. In small bowl, combine dried mushrooms with enough boiling water to cover and set aside for about 20 minutes.
2. In large heavy-gauge skillet, melt 3 tablespoons butter with 1 tablespoon oil over medium-high heat until sizzling. Add 4 pork medallions and sauté 4 to 5 minutes per side.
3. Transfer pork to large platter and cover with foil to keep warm. Repeat step 2 for remaining medallions.
4. Pour off fat, return skillet to medium-high heat, and stir in port, beef stock, and tarragon. Bring liquid to a boil, reduce heat to medium, and cook until reduced by half and slightly thickened, about 15 minutes.
5. While liquid is reducing, rinse limes, if using, and dry. Cut into thin rounds, wrap in plastic, and refrigerate.
6. Drain mushrooms in large strainer and rinse under cold running water to remove any grit. Chop mushrooms finely, wrap them in paper towels, and squeeze out as much moisture as possible.
7. Add mushrooms, tarragon vinegar, and pepper to taste to skillet and cook mixture, stirring, 2 minutes. Remove from heat, cover, and keep warm until ready to serve.
8. Arrange 2 medallions on each dinner plate and remove string. Transfer plates to 200-degree oven to keep pork warm.
9. Just before serving, remove plates from oven and top each medallion with about 2 tablespoons mushroom sauce.

Brussels Sprouts with Ginger

2 pounds Brussels sprouts
2-inch piece fresh ginger root
2 tablespoons unsalted butter
1 teaspoon lemon juice
Salt and freshly ground pepper

1. Wash and trim Brussels sprouts. Grate enough ginger to measure 1 tablespoon.
2. In large saucepan fitted with vegetable steamer, bring small amount of water to a simmer over medium heat.
3. Place Brussels sprouts in steamer and cook, covered, 7 to 10 minutes, or until just tender and green.
4. In large skillet, melt butter over medium heat. Add ginger and Brussels sprouts and cook, tossing, until Brussels sprouts are well coated with butter. Add lemon juice and salt and pepper to taste, and toss again, about 1 minute.
5. Divide Brussels sprouts among 4 plates.

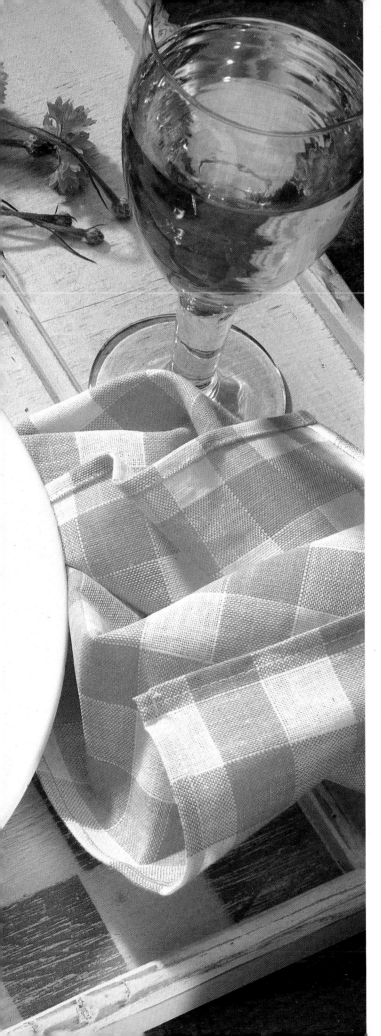

Dennis Gilbert

D ennis Gilbert describes himself as a man who cooks for the love of it and cites his travels through Europe and his experiences as a restaurant chef as the major influences on his culinary style. "Over the years," he says, "I have learned that recipes are really just guidelines and that the best meals can be made by experimenting with the ingredients at hand or by adapting a method to suit the situation." All three of his menus offer cooks the opportunity to be adventurous with a wide range of foods.

In Menu 1, he creates an unlikely—yet delicious—marinade for the country-style ribs by adding orange juice, cumin, coriander seeds, garlic, ginger, and jalapeños to a Japanese plum wine base. The ribs are served with sweet potatoes sautéed in a mildly spiced butter.

He stuffs and rolls slices of pork loin in Menu 2, then braises the rolls in a rich stock with sherry, tomatoes, and okra. For an unusual salad, he combines cucumbers and grapes with a dressing of sour cream, mustard, Japanese green horseradish, and rose water.

Menu 3 is perhaps a bit more traditional but no less interesting. Here Dennis Gilbert sautés medallions of pork tenderloin and tops them with orange sauce for the main course (he says freshly squeezed orange juice is important). The pork goes well with mixed vegetables with green peppercorn sauce and brown rice flavored with scallions, tamari, and sesame oil.

For a casual meal for friends or family, serve country-style ribs with a plum sauce containing red peppers and snow peas. Accompany the ribs with slices of sautéed sweet potato.

Country-style Ribs with Plum Sauce
Sautéed Sweet Potatoes

Japanese plum wine, used in the sauce for the ribs, is a clear, very sweet wine with a delightfully subtle aftertaste of plums. If you prefer, you can substitute a German Gewürztraminer or a sweet Riesling; however, because of their lower alcohol content, these wines do not permit flambéing as the plum wine does. If firm, sweet Italian prune plums are out of season, pitted prunes are an acceptable alternative. They need no prior soaking or softening for this recipe.

Fresh hot jalapeño or the milder Anaheim chilies are increasingly available nationwide. The best are plump and wrinkle-free, without blemishes or soft spots. If you can't find fresh chilies, use red pepper flakes rather than canned chilies.

WHAT TO DRINK

If you choose a Gewürztraminer or Riesling to flavor the pork, serve the same wine with dinner as well. Or try a German *Kabinett*-class Mosel.

SHOPPING LIST AND STAPLES

8 country-style pork ribs, each 1¼ to 1½ inches thick (about 5 pounds total weight)
¼ pound snow peas
2 large red bell peppers (about 1 pound total weight)
2 jalapeño or Anaheim chilies (about 2 ounces total weight), or 1 tablespoon red pepper flakes
4 medium-size sweet potatoes (about 3 pounds total weight)
2 medium-size onions
2 small cloves garlic
Small piece fresh ginger (optional)
4 Italian prune plums, or 6 to 8 pitted prunes
6 tablespoons unsalted butter
3 cups chicken or veal stock, preferably homemade (see page 13), or canned
1 cup fresh orange juice
⅔ cup safflower or sunflower oil, approximately
2 tablespoons arrowroot or cornstarch
½ teaspoon ground cumin
2 teaspoons ground coriander
½ teaspoon ground cardamom
Freshly ground black pepper

¾ cup Japanese plum wine, German Gewürztraminer, or sweet Riesling
¼ cup Scotch whiskey (optional)

UTENSILS

Food processor or blender
Medium-size heavy-gauge saucepan with cover
Large sauté pan with cover
Small sauté pan
Large roasting pan with rack
2 medium-size bowls
3 small bowls
Measuring cups and spoons
Chef's knife
Paring knife
Wooden spoon
Spatula
Fine sieve
Pastry brush
Tongs
Vegetable peeler
Rubber gloves

START-TO-FINISH STEPS

1. Follow ribs recipe step 1.
2. Peel and chop onions for ribs and sweet potatoes recipes. Peel garlic. Mince one clove for ribs recipe and crush remaining clove with chef's knife for sweet potatoes recipe.
3. Follow ribs recipe steps 2 through 5.
4. Follow sweet potatoes recipe step 1.
5. Follow ribs recipe steps 6 and 7.
6. Follow sweet potatoes recipe step 2.
7. Follow ribs recipe steps 8 through 11.
8. Follow sweet potatoes recipe steps 3 through 5.
9. Follow ribs recipe step 12, sweet potatoes recipe step 6, and serve.

RECIPES

Country-style Ribs with Plum Sauce

⅔ cup safflower or sunflower oil, approximately
1 cup fresh orange juice
8 country-style pork ribs, each 1¼ to 1½ inches thick (about 5 pounds total weight)

Freshly ground black pepper
2 large red bell peppers (about 1 pound total weight)
¼ pound snow peas
Small piece fresh ginger (optional)
Medium-size onion, peeled and chopped
¾ cup Japanese plum wine, German Gewürztraminer, or sweet Riesling
3 cups chicken or veal stock
½ teaspoon ground cumin
2 teaspoons ground coriander
2 jalapeño or Anaheim chilies (about 2 ounces total weight), or 1 tablespoon red pepper flakes
4 Italian prune plums, or 6 to 8 pitted prunes
2 tablespoons arrowroot or cornstarch
1 teaspoon minced garlic

1. Preheat oven to 450 degrees.
2. In small bowl, combine ¼ cup of the oil and ⅓ cup of the orange juice.
3. Brush each rib with about 1 teaspoon of remaining oil and season with pepper. Place ribs on rack in roasting pan and cook, turning ribs with tongs 3 or 4 times and basting them with juice mixture, 40 minutes.
4. While ribs are cooking, wash red bell peppers and dry with paper towels. Halve, core, and seed peppers. Cut one pepper into strips and chop remaining pepper. Trim and string snow peas. If using ginger, peel and mince enough to measure 1 teaspoon.
5. Heat 2 tablespoons oil in medium-size heavy-gauge saucepan over medium heat. Add onion and chopped red bell pepper, and sauté until onion is translucent and pepper is soft, about 5 minutes.
6. Remove pan from heat. Add ¼ cup of the plum wine and, averting your face, carefully ignite. When flame subsides, return pan to heat, add stock, remaining ⅔ cup orange juice, cumin, and coriander, and bring to a boil over high heat, skimming off any froth. Reduce heat to low and simmer until reduced to about 2½ cups, about 15 minutes.
7. While sauce is reducing, wearing rubber gloves, cut chilies, if using, into ½-inch-thick rings and remove seeds. Halve and pit plums or prunes, then cut into wedges. In medium-size bowl, combine plums or prunes with chilies, if using, and pepper strips, and toss mixture with ¼ cup plum wine.
8. When sauce is reduced, pass it through fine sieve set over medium-size bowl, pressing on solids to extract as much liquid as possible; discard solids. Return sauce to pan, set over low heat, and add snow peas.
9. Meanwhile, blend arrowroot or cornstarch with remaining ¼ cup plum wine in small bowl and slowly add to sauce, stirring, until sauce thickens, about 1 minute.
10. Add minced garlic and red pepper flakes and ginger, if using, and stir in pepper and plum mixture. Cover pan and set aside in warm place.
11. Place dinner plates under hot running water to warm.
12. Dry plates. Remove ribs from oven. Divide ribs among plates and top each serving with sauce, fruit, and vegetables.

Sautéed Sweet Potatoes

4 medium-size sweet potatoes (about 3 pounds total weight)
6 tablespoons unsalted butter
Medium-size onion, peeled and chopped
Small clove garlic, crushed
½ teaspoon ground cardamom
¼ cup Scotch whiskey (optional)

1. Peel sweet potatoes and cut into ¼-inch-thick rounds.
2. In large sauté pan, melt 2 tablespoons butter over medium-high heat until sizzling. Add sweet potatoes and sauté, turning frequently, until brown on both sides, 8 to 10 minutes.
3. While sweet potatoes are sautéing, melt 2 tablespoons of the butter over medium-low heat in small sauté pan. Add onion and garlic, and cook, stirring, until soft, 3 to 4 minutes.
4. Add remaining butter to onion mixture, sprinkle with cardamom, and carefully pour in Scotch, if using. Cook just until butter melts, about 2 minutes.
5. Transfer onion mixture to food processor or blender and purée. Pour purée over sweet potatoes and cover pan. Reduce heat to very low and cook 3 to 5 minutes, or until fork-tender.
6. Divide sweet potatoes among plates and top each serving with onion purée.

ADDED TOUCH

The knobby Jerusalem artichoke, or sunchoke, a native American vegetable, is the root of one type of sunflower. Available year-round at health food stores and many supermarkets, Jerusalem artichokes are at their best in winter. Before using, scrub them with a brush under cold water.

Stir-Fried Celery and Mushrooms with Jerusalem Artichokes

6 to 8 large celery stalks
½ pound small white mushrooms
½ pound Jerusalem artichokes
2 large shallots
2 tablespoons peanut oil
1 tablespoon clarified butter (see page 12)
¼ cup good-quality dry sherry

1. Trim celery stalks; wash, and dry with paper towels. Cut stalks into crescents ½ inch wide and 2 inches long.
2. Trim mushrooms and wipe clean with damp paper towels.
3. Scrub artichokes well and cut into ¼-inch-thick slices. Peel and chop shallots.
4. In wok or medium-size sauté pan, heat peanut oil over high heat until smoking. Add clarified butter, celery, and mushrooms, and stir fry until mushrooms are golden and celery is bright green, 2 to 3 minutes.
5. Add shallots and sherry, and cook 1 minute. Add artichokes, toss briefly, and serve.

Tangy Cucumber and Grape Salad
Stuffed Pork Rolls with Tomatoes and Okra

Let your guests help themselves to the cucumber and grape salad and ham- and mushroom-filled pork rolls.

T he pork dish contains okra, a popular southern vegetable brought to America by African slaves in the eighteenth century. A tapered green or white seed pod, okra exudes a thick liquid while cooking that gives substance to sauces. The cook offers a general rule of thumb: The fresher the okra, the greater its thickening potential. Buy tender pods that are no longer than 4 inches and that snap easily. If fresh okra is out of season or not readily available in your area, use frozen okra; however, it may be necessary to thicken the sauce with arrowroot.

An unusual combination of *wasabi* (Japanese green horseradish), rose water, and two types of mustard enriches the sour cream dressing for the refreshing salad. *Wasabi* has a potent flavor, so be careful not to use too much. It is sold as a paste or powder, but the powdered form is preferable because it does not deteriorate (mix with a small amount of water or other liquid or wet ingredient as you need it). Rose water, a distillation of fresh rose petals, is used frequently to perfume Indian and Middle Eastern dishes. Add it sparingly to the dressing. Many

liquor stores, pharmacies, and specialty food shops carry rose water.

WHAT TO DRINK

For this meal, select a young California Zinfandel or a Gamay Beaujolais. If you prefer an imported wine, either a young Chianti or a French Beaujolais would be ideal.

SHOPPING LIST AND STAPLES

Eight 1-inch-thick center loin pork scallops (about 2 to 2½ pounds total weight), pounded thin
¼ pound Westphalian ham
½ pound mushrooms
1½ pounds firm Italian plum tomatoes, or 28-ounce can whole peeled tomatoes
1 pound fresh okra, or two 10-ounce packages frozen
2 large cucumbers

Small bunch chives or scallions
Medium-size onion
2 large shallots
Medium-size clove garlic
½ pound seedless red or green grapes
1 stick unsalted butter, approximately
½ pint sour cream or crème fraîche
½ cup chicken stock, preferably homemade (see page 13), or canned
2 teaspoons rose water (optional)
1 tablespoon Dijon mustard
⅔ cup fresh or dried bread crumbs
2 tablespoons arrowroot or cornstarch (optional)
1 teaspoon wasabi or white horseradish
1 teaspoon dried thyme
1 teaspoon dry mustard
½ teaspoon ground sage
1 bay leaf
Ground nutmeg
Salt
Freshly ground black pepper
½ cup good-quality dry sherry

UTENSILS

Food processor (optional)
Large heavy-gauge skillet or sauté pan with cover
Large saucepan
Small saucepan
Medium-size sauté pan
Serving platter
Small bowl
Colander
Measuring cups and spoons
Chef's knife
Paring knife
2 wooden spoons
Metal tongs
Melon baller (optional)
Vegetable peeler (optional)
Kitchen string or wooden toothpicks

START-TO-FINISH STEPS

One hour ahead: If using frozen okra for the pork recipe, remove from packages and set out at room temperature to thaw.

Fifteen minutes ahead: Clarify enough butter (see page 12) to measure ¼ cup for pork recipe.

1. Follow salad recipe step 1.
2. Follow pork rolls recipe steps 1 through 7.
3. Follow salad recipe step 2.
4. Follow pork rolls recipe step 8.
5. While pork rolls are cooking, follow salad recipe steps 3 through 5.
6. Follow pork rolls recipe steps 9 and 10, and serve with salad.

RECIPES

Tangy Cucumber and Grape Salad

2 large cucumbers
2 to 3 tablespoons salt
½ pound seedless red or green grapes
Small bunch chives or scallions
1 cup sour cream or crème fraîche
1 teaspoon dry mustard
1 tablespoon Dijon mustard
1 teaspoon wasabi or white horseradish
¼ cup chicken stock
2 teaspoons rose water (optional)
Ground nutmeg

1. Halve cucumbers lengthwise and remove seeds with melon baller or teaspoon. Peel cucumbers or score decoratively, if desired, and slice into ½-inch-thick crescents. Place cucumbers in colander, sprinkle with salt, and toss to coat. Place colander in sink to drain cucumbers.
2. Wash grapes and dry; remove stems and discard. Wash chives, dry with paper towels, and chop enough to measure 2 tablespoons.
3. In small bowl, blend sour cream, dry and Dijon mustards, and wasabi. Add stock and rose water, if using, and stir until smooth.
4. Rinse cucumbers under very cold running water. Place them in clean dish towel and gently press out as much liquid as possible; set aside.
5. In serving bowl, combine cucumbers and grapes with sour cream dressing and toss until well coated. Sprinkle with nutmeg and set aside until ready to serve.

Stuffed Pork Rolls with Tomatoes and Okra

1 pound fresh okra, or two 10-ounce packages frozen, thawed
½ pound mushrooms
2 large shallots
Medium-size clove garlic
¼ pound Westphalian ham
Medium-size onion
1½ pounds firm Italian plum tomatoes, or 28-ounce can whole peeled tomatoes, drained
¼ cup clarified unsalted butter, plus 2 tablespoons unclarified
1 teaspoon dried thyme
½ teaspoon ground sage
½ cup dry sherry
⅔ cup fresh or dried bread crumbs
Eight 1-inch-thick center loin pork scallops (about 2 to 2½ pounds total weight), pounded thin
1 bay leaf
¼ cup chicken stock
Freshly ground black pepper
2 tablespoons arrowroot or cornstarch (optional)

1. Remove okra stems and cut crosswise into 1-inch-long pieces. In large saucepan, bring 1 quart water to a boil

over high heat. Blanch okra in boiling water 1 to 2 minutes. Turn into colander and set aside.

2. Trim mushrooms and wipe clean with damp paper towels. Peel shallots and garlic. Combine mushrooms, shallots, and garlic in food processor fitted with steel blade and process briefly until minced. Or, mince these ingredients with chef's knife.

3. Chop ham finely. Peel and chop onion. If using fresh tomatoes, rinse and pat dry. Core, halve, and chop tomatoes. If using canned tomatoes, drain and reserve liquid for another use.

4. In medium-size sauté pan, heat 2 tablespoons clarified butter over medium heat. Add mushroom mixture and sauté, stirring occasionally, until mushrooms are browned and most of liquid has evaporated, about 3 minutes. Add thyme, sage, and ¼ cup sherry. Increase heat to high and cook 1 to 2 minutes, stirring until blended. Remove pan from heat and stir in bread crumbs and ham.

5. Mound about ¼ cup of filling in center of each pork scallop. Fold in sides and roll pork into cylinder, totally enclosing filling. Secure rolls with kitchen string or wooden toothpicks.

6. In large heavy-gauge skillet or sauté pan, heat remaining 2 tablespoons clarified butter over medium-high heat. Add pork rolls and brown quickly on all sides, turning with tongs, about 5 minutes.

7. Stir in onion, tomatoes, 2 tablespoons sherry, bay leaf, and stock. Season with generous grinding of pepper and bring to a boil. Cover pan, reduce heat to low, and cook 5 minutes.

8. Add okra and cook another 10 minutes.

9. Transfer pork rolls to serving platter and remove strings or toothpicks. If cooking liquid is thin, blend 2 tablespoons arrowroot with remaining 2 tablespoons sherry in a cup and gradually stir mixture into sauce. If cooking liquid is sufficiently thick, add remaining 2 tablespoons sherry only and stir until blended.

10. Remove pan from heat and swirl in 2 tablespoons unclarified butter, one at a time. Spoon tomatoes, okra, and sauce over pork rolls.

ADDED TOUCH

For this dish, wild rice is served with carrots and celeriac, a gnarled bewhiskered brown-skinned root that tastes like strong celery. Select a small firm root, scrub it well, and use a sharp paring knife to peel away the tough skin.

Wild Rice with Sautéed Carrots and Celeriac

1 cup wild rice
Medium-size onion
2 tablespoons tamari or soy sauce
1 orange
Small bunch carrots (1 pound total weight)
Small-size celeriac (about 1 pound)
2 tablespoons walnut oil or vegetable oil
½ teaspoon dried marjoram
½ teaspoon ground cumin seeds
¼ cup veal or chicken stock, preferably homemade (see page 13), or canned
3 tablespoons sugar
2 tablespoons unsalted butter
Freshly ground black pepper

1. In medium-size heavy-gauge saucepan, bring 5 cups water to a boil.

2. Meanwhile, place wild rice in strainer and rinse thoroughly under cold running water. Peel onion.

3. Place rice, tamari, and whole onion in pan of water. When water returns to a boil, reduce heat to maintain a brisk simmer and cook rice 30 to 40 minutes, or until tender but slightly *al dente*.

4. While rice is cooking, cut orange in half, reserving one half for another use. Squeeze juice from half of orange and set aside. Peel carrots and cut crosswise on the diagonal into long flat slices. Scrub and peel celeriac. Halve celeriac lengthwise and cut each half into wedges. If center is hollow, trim away any discolored flesh. Cut wedges crosswise into ½-inch-thick slices.

5. In large sauté pan, heat walnut oil over medium heat. Add carrots and celeriac, and sauté, stirring, until color of vegetables begins to deepen, about 3 minutes.

6. Add marjoram, cumin, stock, and orange juice to pan; cover, and cook until vegetables are just tender, about 10 minutes.

7. Remove cover from pan and increase heat to medium-high. Sprinkle sugar over vegetables and stir with wooden spoon. Cook, stirring, about 5 minutes, or until liquid reduces to a glaze. Remove pan from heat and cover to keep warm.

8. Drain wild rice in strainer and discard onion. In medium-size bowl, combine rice with half of vegetables. Add butter and pepper to taste and toss rice mixture until butter melts. Add remaining vegetables to rice and serve.

Pork with Orange Sauce
Braised Leeks, Corn, and Carrots with Green Peppercorn Sauce
Oriental Brown Rice

The rich textures of glazed pork medallions, brown rice, and braised vegetables look appealing on plain dinnerware.

Green peppercorns are available packed in brine or vinegar and require refrigeration after opening. The former will keep for about a week, the latter two to three weeks. If the peppercorns turn dark, it means oxidation has occurred, and they should be discarded. Freeze-dried peppercorns do not have the right texture for this recipe.

WHAT TO DRINK

A fruity, slightly off-dry white wine, such as a California Chenin Blanc or a German Riesling from the Rhine valley, is a good choice for this menu.

SHOPPING LIST AND STAPLES

2 pork tenderloins (4 to 5 pounds total weight), trimmed and cut into 1-inch-thick medallions
¼ pound cultivated mushrooms
8 medium-size leeks (about 2 pounds total weight)
3 carrots (about ¾ pound total weight)
Small bunch celery
1 ear of corn, or 10-ounce package frozen corn kernels
1 bunch scallions
Small bunch parsley (optional)
2 medium-size cloves garlic

2 large shallots
6 medium-size oranges
2 lemons
½ pint heavy cream
1 stick plus 2 tablespoons unsalted butter, approximately
1 cup beef or veal stock, preferably homemade (see page 13), or canned, plus ½ cup chicken or veal stock
2-ounce can green peppercorns, packed in brine
2 teaspoons sesame oil
3 tablespoons tamari or soy sauce
2 tablespoons honey
1½ cups short-grain brown rice
2 teaspoons ground coriander
½ teaspoon dried tarragon
½ teaspoon dried thyme
1 bay leaf
Dash of Cayenne pepper
¼ cup dry white wine
2 tablespoons Madeira

UTENSILS

Large heavy-gauge skillet or sauté pan
2 medium-size heavy-gauge saucepans, 1 with cover
Small saucepan
Medium-size sauté pan with cover
Large bowl
Large sieve
Strainer
Measuring cups and spoons
Chef's knife
Paring knife
2 wooden spoons
Spatula
Juicer
Vegetable peeler
Zester (optional)
Tongs

START-TO-FINISH STEPS

One hour ahead: If using frozen corn for leeks recipe, remove from package to thaw.

Fifteen minutes ahead: Clarify enough butter (see page 12) to measure 2 tablespoons for pork recipe.

1. Scrape carrots for pork and leeks recipes.
2. Follow pork recipe steps 1 through 4.
3. While stock is reducing, follow leeks recipe steps 1 and 2.
4. Follow rice recipe steps 1 and 2.
5. Follow pork recipe step 5 and rice recipe step 3.
6. Follow pork recipe steps 6 through 8.
7. While pork is cooking, follow leeks recipe steps 3 through 5.
8. Follow pork recipe step 9 and leeks recipe steps 6 and 7.
9. Follow pork recipe step 10, rice recipe step 4, and serve with leeks.

RECIPES

Pork with Orange Sauce

6 medium-size oranges
¼ pound cultivated mushrooms
1 carrot, scraped
1 celery stalk
2 large shallots
Medium-size clove garlic
Small bunch parsley for garnish (optional)
1 cup beef or veal stock
1 bay leaf
2 teaspoons ground coriander
Dash of Cayenne
1 cup heavy cream
2 tablespoons clarified butter
2 pork tenderloins (4 to 5 pounds total weight), trimmed and cut into 1-inch-thick medallions
¼ cup dry white wine

1. Halve 5 oranges and squeeze enough juice to measure 2 cups. In medium-size heavy-gauge saucepan, boil orange juice over medium-high heat until reduced by half, about 10 minutes.
2. While orange juice is reducing, trim mushrooms, wipe clean with damp paper towels, and chop. Chop carrot. Trim celery, wash, dry with paper towels, and chop. Peel and finely chop shallots. Peel garlic and crush lightly under blade of chef's knife. Peel remaining orange and cut into segments. Wash parsley, if using for garnish, and dry with paper towels. Reserve 4 sprigs and refrigerate remainder for another use.
3. Add stock, mushrooms, celery, shallots, garlic, bay leaf, coriander, and Cayenne to orange juice and continue boiling over medium-high heat until liquid is reduced to about 1 cup, 10 to 15 minutes.
4. Preheat oven to 200 degrees.
5. Add cream, reduce heat to medium, and cook 5 to 7 minutes, or until sauce thickens slightly.
6. Strain sauce into large bowl, pressing on solids with back of spoon to extract as much liquid as possible; discard solids and reserve sauce.
7. Place 4 dinner plates in oven to warm.
8. In large heavy-gauge skillet or sauté pan, heat clarified butter over high heat just until it begins to smoke, about 1 minute. Add pork and brown quickly on all sides, turning with tongs, about 2 minutes. Reduce heat to medium and sauté, turning occasionally, until pork is cooked through, 8 to 10 minutes.
9. Transfer medallions to warm plates. Add white wine to pan and boil over medium-high heat, scraping up any browned bits clinging to bottom of pan, 3 to 4 minutes, or until reduced to about 2 tablespoons.
10. Add reserved sauce and orange segments to pan, and cook sauce over medium heat, stirring frequently, until slightly thickened. Spoon sauce over medallions and garnish each serving with orange segment and parsley sprig, if desired.

Braised Leeks, Corn, and Carrots with Green Peppercorn Sauce

8 medium-size leeks (about 2 pounds total weight)
2 carrots, scraped
2 lemons
Medium-size clove garlic
1 ear of corn, or 10-ounce package frozen corn kernels, thawed
7 tablespoons unsalted butter
½ cup chicken or veal stock
2 tablespoons Madeira
½ teaspoon dried tarragon
½ teaspoon dried thyme
1 tablespoon green peppercorns, packed in brine
2 tablespoons honey

1. Trim green stems from leeks and reserve for another use. Split white parts lengthwise, wash thoroughly in cold water, and dry with paper towels. Cut leeks into 3-inch sections, and cut each section into ¼-inch-thick strips. Cut carrots into fine julienne. Remove zest from lemons and cut into thin strips. Juice lemons and strain juice. Peel and mince garlic.
2. If using fresh corn, remove husks and silk. Trim stem end so upended ear will rest flat on work surface. Holding ear upright, press base against surface and, with chef's knife, cut off kernels by pressing blade against cob and slicing downward. Turn corn and repeat process until all kernels are removed (see illustration on page 34).
3. In medium-size sauté pan, heat 3 tablespoons butter over medium heat until sizzling, about 1 minute. Add leeks and sauté, shaking pan occasionally, until they begin to wilt and are cooked evenly, 3 to 4 minutes.
4. Add lemon juice and zest, stock, Madeira, tarragon, and thyme. Reduce heat to low, until liquid barely simmers, then add corn and carrots. Cover pan and braise vegetables just until tender, 4 to 5 minutes.
5. Meanwhile, place peppercorns in strainer and rinse under cold running water to remove brine.
6. Transfer leeks to warm plates. Remove any tough outer layers of leek strips. Add honey to pan, increase heat to medium-high, and boil 1 to 2 minutes, or until sauce begins to shine.
7. Remove pan from heat and add garlic and green peppercorns. Still off heat, swirl in remaining butter, one tablespoon at a time. Spoon sauce over leeks and serve.

Oriental Brown Rice

1½ cups short-grain brown rice
3 tablespoons tamari or soy sauce
2 teaspoons sesame oil
1 bunch scallions

1. Place rice in large sieve and rinse well under cold running water.
2. In medium-size heavy-gauge saucepan, combine rice, 2⅔ cups water, tamari, and sesame oil. Cover pan and bring to a boil over high heat. Reduce heat to medium-low

so water maintains a brisk simmer and cook until rice is tender but not soft, about 35 minutes.
3. Trim scallions, wash, and dry with paper towels. Chop enough scallions to measure ½ cup.
4. Just before serving, toss rice with chopped scallions and divide among warm plates.

ADDED TOUCH

You can use fresh raspberries rather than frozen ones for the sauce: Macerate 1 cup of fresh berries with 3 tablespoons of sugar and 1 tablespoon of Drambuie for an hour or two, then purée the berries and strain out the seeds.

Lemon Mousse with Tropical Fruits and Raspberry Sauce

3 lemons
1 orange
3 tablespoons Drambuie
1 package (1 tablespoon) unflavored gelatin
1 ripe mango
1 large kiwi, or 2 small
3 eggs
½ cup plus 3 tablespoons sugar
1 cup heavy cream
8-ounce package frozen raspberries, thawed

1. Place large bowl and beaters in refrigerator to chill. Grate zest of 2 lemons and orange into small saucepan. Squeeze enough lemon juice to measure ½ cup and strain juice. If necessary to make ½ cup juice, squeeze orange and add to lemon juice. Add juice, Drambuie, and gelatin to pan and set aside to soften.
2. Peel mango and remove flesh. Chop fruit into small dice and set aside in strainer to drain. Peel kiwi, cut crosswise into ¼-inch-thick slices, and set aside.
3. Bring juice mixture to a simmer over low heat until gelatin dissolves, 1 to 2 minutes. Pour mixture into medium-size bowl, cover, and refrigerate until cooled, about 10 minutes.
4. Meanwhile, separate eggs, placing yolks and whites in separate bowls.
5. With whisk, beat egg yolks with ½ cup sugar until thick and lemon colored. Wash and dry whisk.
6. Add remaining 3 tablespoons sugar to egg whites and whisk until stiff.
7. When gelatin mixture is cool but not set, add to yolks and stir to combine.
8. In large chilled bowl, beat heavy cream with electric mixer set at high speed until it holds a soft shape.
9. With rubber spatula, fold yolk mixture into whites. Gently fold this mixture into cream until no streaks show.
10. Divide mango among 4 stemmed glasses and top with spoonful of mousse. Cover with slices of kiwi and top with remaining mousse. Cover with plastic wrap and refrigerate until chilled and set, at least 1 hour.
11. Just before serving, purée raspberries in blender or food processor and then strain them. Top each mousse with a spoonful of raspberry sauce.

Meryle Evans

MENU 1 (Left)
Smoked Salmon with Dilled Crème Fraîche
Cucumber Salad
Prune-Stuffed Pork Chops with Apples
Spinach Pancakes

MENU 2
Ham Steak with Maple-Bourbon Glaze
Ambrosia
Individual Spoonbreads

MENU 3
Oysters on the Half Shell
Jambalaya
Artichoke Hearts with Creole Rémoulade

An authority on American regional cooking, Meryle Evans feels that two important factors shaped this country's cuisine: the presence of indigenous ingredients such as pumpkins, cranberries, sweet corn, and maple syrup, and the arrival of immigrants bringing traditional recipes from many countries. Two of this cook's menus reflect her strong interest in American food, and the third is Scandinavian, a cuisine she has been studying recently.

Menu 2 is a traditional southern meal that can be prepared in very little time. It features ham steak glazed with maple syrup and bourbon, and individual cornmeal spoonbreads. With the pork Meryle Evans serves ambrosia, a sweet concoction of fruit and coconut that was created in the nineteenth century.

She offers a Creole dinner from New Orleans in Menu 3. The main course, jambalaya (the name comes from the French *jambon*, meaning ham), is a blend of French, Spanish, African, and American influences, as is most Creole food. This jambalaya includes ham, sausage, shrimp, vegetables, and rice, and is served with artichoke hearts and Creole *rémoulade*.

Menu 1 focuses on Scandinavian dishes. Pork chops stuffed with prunes is a variation on a Swedish specialty, prune-stuffed pork loin. It is served with Finnish spinach pancakes, smoked salmon (preferably Norwegian), and a refreshing cucumber salad.

Prune-stuffed pork chops with zesty sautéed apples spooned on top and spinach pancakes make an ample main course for this Scandinavian meal. Offer the sliced-cucumber salad with sprigs of fresh dill, and the smoked salmon rolls with a spoonful of crème fraîche.

Smoked Salmon with Dilled Crème Fraîche / Cucumber Salad
Prune-Stuffed Pork Chops with Apples
Spinach Pancakes

Smoked salmon is an elegant first course by itself or is equally delicious served, as here, with a cucumber salad. Buy top-quality salmon, such as Norwegian, Scotch, Irish, or Nova Scotia, and have it sliced paper thin. Salmon is perishable, so refrigerate it and use it quickly. *Crème fraîche*, which tops each serving of salmon, is thick, naturally fermented cream (see the start-to-finish steps for a simple recipe). It is occasionally available in the dairy section of well-stocked supermarkets. Sour cream is an acceptable substitute.

Try some *crème fraîche* on the spinach pancakes, or top them with melted butter.

WHAT TO DRINK

Cold aquavit is a fitting aperitif here. With the meal, offer Riesling—a lightly sweet *Kabinett* from Germany, a dry balanced bottle from Alsace, or a full-bodied one from California.

SHOPPING LIST AND STAPLES

Four ¾-inch-thick loin pork chops (about 2 pounds total weight) with pockets cut in sides for stuffing
12 thin slices smoked salmon, preferably Norwegian (about ⅓ pound total weight)
2 large cucumbers
Small head Boston or Bibb lettuce
½ pound fresh spinach
Large bunch dill
2 large firm tart apples, such as Granny Smith
1 lemon
2 eggs
1¼ cups milk
½ cup crème fraîche, preferably homemade, or commercial
1 stick plus 2 tablespoons unsalted butter
⅔ cup red or white wine vinegar
1 tablespoon Dijon mustard
8-ounce box medium-size pitted prunes
1 cup all-purpose flour
2 tablespoons plus ½ teaspoon granulated sugar
2 tablespoons light brown sugar
Ground nutmeg
Ground cloves
Salt

Freshly ground white pepper
Freshly ground black pepper

UTENSILS

Food processor or blender
Large heavy-gauge skillet with cover plus additional skillet (if not using griddle)
Griddle (optional)
Small heavy-gauge saucepan or butter warmer
13 x 9-inch shallow, ovenproof casserole or baking dish
Large bowl
2 medium-size bowls
Small bowl
Large sieve or strainer
Measuring cups and spoons
Chef's knife
Paring knife
2 wooden spoons
Slotted spoon
Metal spatula or pancake turner
Rubber spatula
Tongs
Wooden toothpicks or small metal skewers

START-TO-FINISH STEPS

The day before: If using homemade crème fraîche for salmon recipe, prepare as follows: Whisk ½ pint heavy cream into ½ pint sour cream at room temperature. Pour mixture into glass jar and cover tightly; let stand in warm place for 6 to 8 hours, then refrigerate.

Thirty minutes ahead: Soak prunes in hot water to cover.

1. Wash, dry, and mince dill for salmon and cucumber salad recipes.
2. Follow cucumber salad recipe steps 1 and 2.
3. Follow pork chops recipe steps 1 through 7.
4. Follow cucumber salad recipe step 3.
5. Follow pork chops recipe step 8 and pancakes recipe steps 1 through 4.
6. Follow salmon recipe steps 1 and 2, cucumber salad recipe step 4, and serve as appetizer.
7. While chops are still baking, follow pork chops recipe step 9 and pancakes recipe step 5.
8. Follow pork chops recipe step 10, and serve with pancakes.

RECIPES

Smoked Salmon with Dilled Crème Fraîche

½ cup crème fraîche, preferably homemade, or
    commercial
1 tablespoon minced dill plus 4 dill sprigs for garnish
    (optional)
12 thin slices smoked salmon, preferably Norwegian
    (about ⅓ pound total weight)

1. In small bowl, blend crème fraîche and minced dill.
2. Roll up slices of smoked salmon and arrange 3 rolls on each of 4 salad plates, leaving room for cucumber salad. Top each serving with spoonful of dilled crème fraîche and garnish each with dill sprig, if desired. Cover and refrigerate until ready to serve.

Cucumber Salad

⅔ cup red or white wine vinegar
2 tablespoons sugar
1 teaspoon salt
½ teaspoon freshly ground white pepper
2 large cucumbers
¼ cup minced dill plus 4 dill sprigs for garnish (optional)
Small head Boston or Bibb lettuce

1. In medium-size bowl, combine vinegar, sugar, salt, pepper, and ⅓ cup ice water.
2. Peel cucumbers and slice thinly. Add slices to bowl and stir. Sprinkle cucumbers with dill, cover, and refrigerate until ready to serve.
3. Wash lettuce and dry with paper towels. Wrap in paper towels and refrigerate until ready to serve.
4. Arrange lettuce leaves on plates with salmon and top with cucumbers; garnish with dill sprigs, if desired.

Prune-Stuffed Pork Chops with Apples

8 medium-size pitted prunes, soaked in hot water for 30
    minutes
Four ¾-inch-thick loin pork chops (about 2 pounds total
    weight) with pockets cut in sides for stuffing
Salt and freshly ground black pepper
1 lemon
2 large firm tart apples, such as Granny Smith
6 tablespoons unsalted butter
2 tablespoons light brown sugar
½ teaspoon ground nutmeg
Pinch of ground cloves
1 tablespoon Dijon mustard

1. Preheat oven to 350 degrees.
2. Stuff 2 soft prunes into each pork chop pocket and secure pocket with toothpick or small skewer. Rub both sides of each chop with salt and pepper.
3. Grate enough lemon zest to make 2 teaspoons and set aside. Cut lemon in half and squeeze juice from both halves into large bowl. Wash apples under cold running water. Halve 1 apple, core, and cut into 8 thin slices. Peel, core, and coarsely chop remaining apple. Toss apple slices

and chunks in lemon juice to prevent discoloration, and set aside.
4. In large heavy-gauge skillet, melt 2 tablespoons butter over medium-high heat until frothy, about 1 minute. Add chops and sauté, turning once, until well browned, 3 to 4 minutes per side.
5. Transfer chops to shallow, ovenproof casserole or baking dish; set aside. Wipe out skillet with paper towels.
6. In skillet, melt remaining butter over medium heat. With slotted spoon, remove apple chunks from lemon juice and dry with paper towels; reserve the apple slices. Add chunks to skillet, tossing until evenly coated with butter. Cover and cook until apples are slightly soft, 2 to 3 minutes.
7. Stir in lemon zest, light brown sugar, nutmeg, cloves, and pinch of salt, and cook about 5 minutes, or until ingredients are combined. Stir in mustard.
8. Spoon half of apple mixture over chops and bake 30 to 40 minutes, or until no pink shows at the bone and apples are golden brown. Cover remaining apple mixture and set aside.
9. Place 4 dinner plates under hot running water to warm.
10. Dry plates. Divide chops among warmed plates and top each serving with spoonful of remaining apple mixture. Garnish each with 2 slices of reserved raw apple slices and serve immediately.

Spinach Pancakes

½ pound fresh spinach
4 tablespoons unsalted butter, approximately
1 cup all-purpose flour
1 teaspoon salt
½ teaspoon sugar
1¼ cups milk
2 eggs

1. Remove tough stems from spinach and discard. Wash spinach thoroughly; do not dry. Transfer to large skillet, cover, and steam over medium heat 4 to 5 minutes, or until wilted.
2. Meanwhile, in small heavy-gauge saucepan or butter warmer, melt butter over low heat.
3. Turn spinach into sieve or strainer and squeeze out as much moisture as possible. Chop finely.
4. In food processor fitted with metal blade or in blender, combine flour, salt, sugar, milk, eggs, and 2 tablespoons melted butter; process until blended. Transfer to medium-size bowl and fold in spinach. Set batter aside.
5. In large skillet or griddle, warm ½ tablespoon melted butter over low heat. When butter begins to foam, pour out about 2 tablespoons batter per pancake, making four 3-inch pancakes. Cook until undersides begin to brown, 2 to 3 minutes. Using metal spatula or pancake turner, turn pancakes and cook other side another minute. Transfer to plate, place square of waxed paper between pancakes, and cover loosely with foil. Repeat with remaining batter, adding butter to pan as needed, to make a total of 12 to 16 pancakes.

Ham Steak with Maple-Bourbon Glaze
Ambrosia
Individual Spoonbreads

Maple-flavored syrup is sold in most supermarkets, but it lacks the intense flavor of pure maple syrup, which is preferred for the ham. Although costly, pure maple syrup is worth the extra money. Store the syrup in the refrigerator once opened because it spoils quickly if left at room temperature.

The spoonbreads, made with cornmeal, milk, and eggs, are more like pudding than bread. The cook prefers using white stoneground meal, available at health food stores and some supermarkets, but regular yellow cornmeal is an acceptable substitute.

WHAT TO DRINK

The cook suggests a dry rosé to accompany this dinner. Try a varietal Cabernet rosé from California or a fine French Tavel.

SHOPPING LIST AND STAPLES

1½-inch-thick center-cut ham steak (about 2½ pounds)
4 medium-size navel oranges
Small bunch seedless green grapes (about ¼ pound)
4 eggs
1 cup milk
4½ tablespoons unsalted butter
¼ cup pure maple syrup
1 teaspoon all-purpose flour
1 cup white or yellow cornmeal, preferably stoneground
Three 4-ounce bags sweetened shredded coconut
2 tablespoons sugar, approximately
Pinch of ground cloves
¼ teaspoon dry mustard
Salt
2 tablespoons bourbon
¼ cup plus 2 tablespoons dry red wine

UTENSILS

Large heavy-gauge skillet
Medium-size heavy-gauge saucepan
Four 10- to 12-ounce ramekins or other small ovenproof
    dishes
2 medium-size bowls
Small bowl
Measuring cups and spoons
Chef's knife
Paring knife

Slices of ham steak with maple-bourbon glaze and sweet ambrosia are the basis of an easy informal supper (the ambrosia could also be served for dessert). Serve the spoonbreads in their individual ramekins.

Wooden spoon
Spatula
Egg beater or electric mixer (optional)
Tongs

START-TO-FINISH STEPS

1. Follow ambrosia recipe steps 1 and 2.
2. Follow spoonbreads recipe steps 1 through 5.
3. Follow ham recipe steps 1 through 4. (If ham is ready before spoonbreads, leave in skillet and reheat briefly just before serving.)
4. Follow ham recipe step 5, ambrosia recipe step 3, and serve with spoonbreads.

RECIPES

Ham Steak with Maple-Bourbon Glaze

1½ tablespoons unsalted butter
1½-inch-thick center-cut ham steak (about 2½ pounds)
Pinch of ground cloves
¼ teaspoon dry mustard
1 teaspoon all-purpose flour
¼ cup plus 2 tablespoons dry red wine
2 tablespoons bourbon
¼ cup pure maple syrup

1. In large heavy-gauge skillet, melt butter over medium heat. Brown ham on both sides, 6 to 7 minutes per side, and transfer to platter. Remove skillet from heat and reserve.
2. In small bowl, combine cloves, dry mustard, flour, and 2 tablespoons water.
3. Return skillet to low heat. Add spice mixture, red wine, bourbon, and maple syrup, and stir until blended. Cook slowly, stirring constantly, until glaze begins to thicken, 1 to 2 minutes.
4. Return ham to skillet and heat through, turning once or twice, about 8 minutes.
5. Transfer ham to cutting board and slice crosswise. Arrange 3 to 4 slices on each of 4 dinner plates and top with glaze.

Ambrosia

4 medium-size navel oranges
Small bunch seedless green grapes (about ¼ pound)
2 tablespoons sugar, approximately
1½ cups sweetened shredded coconut

1. With paring knife, peel oranges and remove white pith. Cut crosswise into ¼-inch-thick rounds. Wash grapes and dry with paper towels.
2. Place orange slices and grapes in medium-size bowl. If oranges are tart, sprinkle with a little sugar. Cover and refrigerate until ready to serve.
3. Just before serving, overlap 3 to 4 orange slices on each dinner plate and sprinkle with coconut. Scatter grapes over the slices.

Individual Spoonbreads

1 cup white or yellow cornmeal, preferably
    stoneground
1 teaspoon salt
3 tablespoons unsalted butter
4 eggs
1 cup milk

1. Preheat oven to 425 degrees. Lightly grease four 10- to 12-ounce ramekins or other ovenproof dishes.
2. In medium-size saucepan, combine cornmeal and salt. Add 2 cups boiling water and stir well. Cook over medium heat, stirring constantly, 1 to 2 minutes, or until thickened.
3. Remove pan from heat and add butter, stirring until melted.
4. In medium-size bowl, beat eggs until frothy and lemon colored. Add milk and stir until blended. Add egg mixture to cornmeal mixture and stir until batter is smooth.
5. Divide batter among ramekins and bake about 25 minutes, or until tip of knife inserted in center comes out clean.

ADDED TOUCH

For this quick-to-assemble hearty salad, you can use canned black-eyed peas instead of frozen, but be sure to drain them well.

Black-Eyed Pea Salad

10-ounce package frozen black-eyed peas
Small head Boston or Bibb lettuce
2 medium-size tomatoes (about 1 pound total weight)
2 stalks celery
Small red onion (optional)
⅓ cup corn oil
3 to 4 tablespoons red or white wine vinegar
½ teaspoon dry mustard
Salt
Freshly ground pepper

1. In medium-size saucepan, cook peas as directed on package. Drain, transfer to medium-size bowl, cover, and refrigerate until chilled.
2. Meanwhile, wash lettuce and dry in salad spinner or with paper towels. Wrap in paper towels and refrigerate.
3. Wash tomatoes and celery, and dry with paper towels. Core, halve, and coarsely chop tomatoes; finely chop enough celery to measure 1 cup. Set aside.
4. If using red onion, peel and mince enough to measure 1 tablespoon; set aside.
5. In small bowl, whisk corn oil, vinegar, dry mustard, and salt and pepper to taste until blended.
6. Add tomatoes, celery, and onion, if using, to peas and toss to combine. Add vinaigrette and toss until evenly coated.
7. Divide lettuce among salad plates, top with salad, and serve.

Oysters on the Half Shell
Jambalaya
Artichoke Hearts with Creole Rémoulade

Oysters on the half shell introduce the hearty jambalaya, accompanied by artichoke hearts on a bed of watercress.

Raw oysters on the half shell require little preparation. Buy them as close to serving time as possible to preserve their freshness.

WHAT TO DRINK

With this meal, serve a fruity but firm red wine such as a young California Zinfandel or an Italian Barbera or Dolcetto.

SHOPPING LIST AND STAPLES

4 spicy link sausages, such as Polish or Italian (about 10 ounces total weight)
½ pound precooked ham
½ pound medium-size shrimp
12 oysters
Large bunch watercress
Large green bell pepper
Large stalk celery
2 medium-large onions
Small bunch scallions
2 cloves garlic
Small bunch parsley
1 lemon plus additional lemon (optional)
3 tablespoons unsalted butter, bacon fat, or lard
16-ounce can Italian plum tomatoes
2 cups chicken stock, preferably homemade (see page 13), or canned
Two 14-ounce cans water-packed artichoke hearts
⅓ cup vegetable oil
⅓ cup olive oil
¼ cup red or white wine vinegar
1 tablespoon Creole or Dijon mustard
1 tablespoon prepared horseradish
1 cup long-grain rice
¼ teaspoon dried thyme
1 teaspoon paprika
¼ teaspoon Cayenne pepper
Pinch of ground cloves
Salt and freshly ground black pepper
2 tablespoons anise-flavored liqueur, such as Pernod

Food processor or blender (optional)
Large heavy-gauge skillet with cover
Small bowl
Salad spinner (optional)
Measuring cups and spoons
Chef's knife
Paring knife
Serrated knife
Wooden spoon
Tongs
Oyster knife (optional)
Pastry brush

START-TO-FINISH STEPS

Two hours ahead: Refrigerate artichoke hearts.

1. Wash parsley and watercress; dry in salad spinner or with paper towels. Remove stems from watercress and discard. Wrap in paper towels and refrigerate. Mince enough parsley to measure 6 tablespoons; set aside. Rinse 1 lemon, dry with paper towel, and cut crosswise into 8 rounds; set aside. Juice remaining lemon.
2. Follow oysters recipe steps 1 and 2.
3. Follow jambalaya recipe steps 1 through 7.
4. While jambalaya is cooking, serve oysters.
5. Follow artichoke hearts recipe steps 1 through 3.
6. Follow jambalaya recipe step 8 and serve with artichoke hearts.

RECIPES

Oysters on the Half Shell

12 oysters
2 tablespoons anise-flavored liqueur, such as Pernod
1 lemon for garnish
Watercress for garnish

1. Shuck oysters, reserving liquor and bottom shells.
2. Arrange 3 oysters on each of 4 salad plates, top with a spoonful of reserved liquor, and brush lightly with anise liqueur. Garnish each serving with 2 lemon slices and watercress, cover, and refrigerate until ready to serve.

Jambalaya

4 spicy link sausages, such as Polish or Italian, (about 10 ounces total weight)
½ pound precooked ham
Large green bell pepper
Large stalk celery
2 medium-large onions
2 cloves garlic
3 tablespoons unsalted butter, bacon fat, or lard
¼ cup minced fresh parsley
¼ teaspoon dried thyme
¼ teaspoon Cayenne pepper

¼ teaspoon freshly ground black pepper
Pinch of ground cloves
½ pound medium-size shrimp
2 cups canned Italian plum tomatoes, with juice
2 cups chicken stock
1 cup long-grain rice

1. Cut sausages into ½-inch pieces and dice enough ham to measure 1 cup; set aside.
2. Wash bell pepper and celery; dry with paper towels. Halve, core, seed, and coarsely chop pepper; chop celery. Peel and chop onions; peel and mince garlic.
3. In large heavy-gauge skillet, melt butter over medium heat. Add sausages and ham, and sauté 5 to 7 minutes, or until sausage is browned.
4. Meanwhile, peel and devein shrimp: Starting at head end, slip thumb under shell between feelers. Lift off 2 or 3 shell segments at once and, holding tail, pull shrimp out of shell. Pull off tail shell. With sharp paring knife, slit down back and lift out black vein.
5. Add green bell pepper, celery, onions, garlic, and 2 tablespoons of the parsley to skillet, and cook, stirring frequently, until onions are soft and translucent, about 5 minutes.
6. Stir in thyme, Cayenne, black pepper, cloves, and shrimp. Add tomatoes and chicken stock, and bring to a boil.
7. Add rice, reduce heat to a gentle simmer, cover, and cook, stirring occasionally, until rice is tender, 25 to 30 minutes.
8. Divide jambalaya among dinner plates and garnish with remaining parsley. Serve at once.

Artichoke Hearts with Creole Rémoulade

Small bunch scallions
1 tablespoon Creole or Dijon mustard
1 tablespoon prepared horseradish
¼ cup red or white wine vinegar
Juice of 1 lemon
1 teaspoon paprika
⅓ cup vegetable oil
⅓ cup olive oil
2 tablespoons minced parsley
Salt and freshly ground pepper
Large bunch watercress
Two 14-ounce cans water-packed artichoke hearts, chilled

1. Wash scallions and dry with paper towels. Trim off root ends and chop enough to measure ½ cup; set aside.
2. In food processor or blender, combine mustard, horseradish, vinegar, lemon juice, and paprika. Process, adding vegetable and olive oils in a slow, steady stream, until sauce is thick and smooth. Turn sauce into small bowl and stir in scallions and parsley. Add salt and pepper to taste, cover, and chill in freezer until ready to serve.
3. Divide watercress among 4 dinner plates. Drain artichoke hearts, cut in half, and arrange on top of watercress. Top each serving with a spoonful of Creole rémoulade.

Lee Haiken

After many years of cooking professionally and for her own pleasure, Lee Haiken has eliminated elaborate, time-consuming menus from her repertoire. She advocates meals that are simply seasoned and judiciously sauced, and she carefully selects seasonal produce and basic staples for their nutritional content. Today's lean pork often turns up on her table.

When she does occasionally prepare a rich menu—such as the French regional dishes of Menu 2—she makes sure that it is well balanced and wholesome. This dinner features a Normandy-style entrée of sautéed pork with apples and cream sauce over spinach noodles, and button mushrooms on garlic-flavored toast triangles as the appetizer. Julienne celery, thinly sliced radishes, and Gruyère cheese are tossed with a Dijon-mustard vinaigrette for the salad.

Her Menu 1 is a lighter meal. Swiss chard leaves (high in vitamin A) are wrapped around a filling of pork and bulgur, a wheat product rich in B-complex vitamins. The dilled carrots are cooked briefly to retain their texture and provide a colorful contrast to the pork rolls.

Menu 3 is a festive south-of-the-border dinner for family or guests. Cubed pork is simmered with green chilies, fresh coriander, and cumin, and served with tortillas and cooling slices of ripe tomato. The avocado and grapefruit salad may be served before or with the meal.

A patterned tablecloth suits the varied textures of this Eastern European-style meal. To serve, mound the dilled carrots in the center of a large round platter and surround them with stuffed chard leaves. Offer the herb bread and a cucumber and onion salad on the side.

Sweet Onion and Cucumber Salad
Pork-Stuffed Swiss Chard Rolls
Dilled Carrots / Herb Bread

An underutilized vegetable, chard—commonly called Swiss chard—is more like two vegetables than one: Its leaves resemble spinach, and its white stems (which are not used in this recipe) can be cooked like celery or asparagus. Look for chard with crisp leaves. Use a pot large enough to accommodate the chard leaves because they break easily, and blanch them one at a time; then cook the carrots in the same water to heighten their flavor.

WHAT TO DRINK

Try a crisp dry white wine such as a California or Italian Sauvignon Blanc or French Sancerre with this meal.

SHOPPING LIST AND STAPLES

1 pound ground fresh pork
2 large sweet onions, such as Bermuda
Small bunch medium-size carrots (about 1 pound)
2 large cucumbers
1 bunch Swiss chard (about ½ pound), or medium-size head Napa cabbage
Small bunch fresh parsley
Small bunch fresh chives, or 2 tablespoons plus 2 teaspoons frozen
Small bunch fresh dill, or 2 teaspoons dried
Small bunch fresh mint, or 1 to 2 teaspoons dried
Small bunch fresh tarragon for garnish (optional)
2 cloves garlic
3 large lemons
4 tablespoons unsalted butter or margarine
6-ounce can tomato juice, or 2 to 4 tablespoons beef or chicken stock
3 tablespoons sesame oil, approximately
½ cup rice wine vinegar or white wine vinegar
¼ teaspoon dry mustard
¼ pound bulgur, approximately
1 long loaf French or Italian bread
½ teaspoon sugar
Salt
Freshly ground black pepper
Freshly ground white pepper

UTENSILS

Stockpot
Medium-size nonstick skillet
Medium-size heavy-gauge saucepan with cover
Large bowl
2 medium-size bowls
Small bowl
Colander
Large strainer
Measuring cups and spoons
Chef's knife
Paring knife
Wooden spoons
Slotted spoon
Spatula
Metal tongs
Vegetable peeler
Juicer
Kitchen scissors

START-TO-FINISH STEPS

Thirty minutes ahead: Set out 4 tablespoons unsalted butter or margarine at room temperature for bread recipe.

1. Prepare parsley and fresh herbs, if using. Prepare onions for pork rolls and for salad. Squeeze enough of 1 lemon to measure 2 tablespoons plus 1 teaspoon juice and thinly slice remaining 2 lemons; set aside.
2. Follow pork recipe steps 1 through 7.
3. Follow salad recipe steps 1 through 3.
4. Follow bread recipe step 1 and carrots recipe steps 1 through 4.
5. Follow bread recipe step 2 and carrots recipe step 5.
6. Follow pork recipe step 8 and bread recipe steps 3 and 4.
7. Serve salad as the first course, if desired.
8. Follow bread recipe step 5, carrots recipe step 6, pork recipe step 9, and serve.

RECIPES

Sweet Onion and Cucumber Salad

2 large cucumbers
3 cups sliced sweet onions, approximately
½ cup rice wine vinegar or white wine vinegar
½ teaspoon sugar
5 sprigs fresh tarragon for garnish (optional)

1. Rinse cucumbers, dry with paper towels. Using fork, score lengthwise, ⅛ inch apart, around full circumference

of cucumber. Then cut crosswise into ¼-inch-thick rounds and place cucumbers in medium-size bowl.

2. Add onions to cucumbers, sprinkle with vinegar and sugar, and toss to combine.

3. Transfer onions and cucumbers to serving plate, garnish with tarragon, if desired, cover with plastic wrap, and refrigerate until ready to serve.

Pork-Stuffed Swiss Chard Rolls

½ cup bulgur
1 bunch Swiss chard (about ½ pound), or medium-size
    head Napa cabbage
1 pound ground fresh pork
¼ cup chopped onion
1 to 2 tablespoons chopped fresh mint, or 1 to 2 teaspoons
    dried
1½ teaspoons salt
½ teaspoon freshly ground black pepper
2 to 4 tablespoons tomato juice or beef or chicken
    stock
1 tablespoon lemon juice
2 lemons, thinly sliced

1. In large bowl, combine bulgur with 1 cup warm tap water, cover, and set aside at least 10 minutes.

2. In stockpot, bring 3 quarts water to a boil over high heat.

3. If using Swiss chard, with scissors, remove stems from 12 leaves, reserving stems and remainder of bunch for another use. At stem end, cut out small V-shaped wedge to facilitate rolling leaf over filling. Blanch each chard leaf, one at a time, in boiling water, 15 to 20 seconds. With slotted spoon, carefully remove each leaf, refresh under cold running water, and drain on paper towels. Or, if using cabbage, blanch whole head in boiling water 5 minutes. Transfer to colander and drain. Peel 12 leaves from head, reserving remainder for another use. Trim off wedge at core end of each leaf and discard. Reserve blanched leaves until ready to use. Set blanching water aside for carrot recipe, if desired.

4. Place ground pork in medium-size nonstick skillet over medium-high heat and sauté, stirring with wooden spoon, 6 to 8 minutes, or until meat turns white. Remove pan from heat; drain off fat and discard.

5. Turn bulgur into large strainer to drain. Dry bowl.

6. In large bowl, combine bulgur, chopped onion, mint, and 1 teaspoon salt. Stir in cooked pork, pepper, and just enough tomato juice or stock to moisten mixture.

7. Near one end of chard or cabbage leaf, spread about 3 tablespoons pork filling. Fold leaf over filling, tuck in sides, and roll up to enclose. Repeat process with remaining leaves. Set aside.

8. In medium-size heavy-gauge saucepan, combine 1 cup water, lemon juice, and remaining salt. Place pork rolls, seam-side down, in pan and top with lemon slices. Bring liquid to a boil over high heat. Cover pan, reduce heat to low, and cook pork rolls 20 minutes, or until heated through.

9. Discard lemon slices and, with slotted spoon, transfer rolls to platter with carrots, and serve.

Dilled Carrots

Small bunch medium-size carrots (about 1 pound)
2 cloves garlic
1 tablespoon lemon juice
¼ teaspoon salt
¼ teaspoon dry mustard
Freshly ground white pepper
2 to 3 tablespoons sesame oil
2 teaspoons chopped fresh or frozen chives
2 tablespoons minced fresh dill, or 2 teaspoons dried

1. In stockpot, bring 3 quarts water, preferably that reserved from blanching chard, to a boil over high heat.

2. While water is heating, trim and scrape carrots; cut on diagonal into ¼-inch-thick slices.

3. Add carrots to boiling water and cook 7 to 8 minutes, or until barely tender when pierced with tip of knife.

4. Meanwhile, peel garlic and halve lengthwise. Rub medium-size bowl with cut sides of garlic and discard. Set bowl aside.

5. Turn carrots into colander to drain and then transfer to bowl. Sprinkle carrots with lemon juice, salt, dry mustard, and white pepper to taste, and toss gently. Gradually add sesame oil, stirring carrots until evenly coated. Cover loosely with foil and set aside until ready to serve.

6. Just before serving, add chives and dill, and toss gently to combine. Transfer carrots to center of serving platter.

Herb Bread

4 tablespoons unsalted butter or margarine, at room
    temperature
2 tablespoons chopped fresh or frozen chives
2 tablespoons chopped fresh parsley
1 teaspoon lemon juice
1 long loaf French or Italian bread

1. Preheat oven to 350 degrees.

2. In small bowl, blend butter, chives, parsley, and lemon juice with wooden spoon.

3. Slice loaf of bread in half lengthwise. Spread herb butter evenly over cut sides of bread. Press halves together to reshape loaf and wrap securely in aluminum foil.

4. Place bread in oven for 10 to 15 minutes, or until warmed through.

5. Just before serving, remove foil from loaf, separate halves, and serve in napkin-lined basket.

LEFTOVER SUGGESTION

Add raw, sliced Swiss chard stems to any vegetable or meat soup, allowing at least 10 minutes' cooking time. Or cut the stems into 1- to 2-inch-long pieces, blanch them, and then stir fry or sauté with other vegetables. The stems can also be cut into 5-inch lengths, then blanched, and served with hollandaise sauce like asparagus.

Sautéed Button Mushrooms on Garlic Toast
Pork and Apples with Spinach Noodles
Celery, Radish, and Gruyère Salad

Button mushrooms on triangles of garlic toast can precede the pork and apples, spinach noodles, and mixed salad.

Select button mushrooms with care, picking them out individually if possible. They should be firm, smooth, and free of blemishes, and the caps should be closed around the stems. To store button mushrooms for several days, spread them out in a single layer on a nonmetal platter and cover with damp paper towels. Never wash fresh cultivated mushrooms or immerse them in water because they will become soggy. Instead, carefully wipe them clean with damp paper towels. For best results, sauté the mushrooms just before serving them on the toast triangles.

Information on the blade Boston pork roast for this menu appears on page 9.

WHAT TO DRINK

This meal calls for a full-bodied white wine. Choose a California Chardonnay or a simple French Chablis.

SHOPPING LIST AND STAPLES

1½ pounds blade Boston pork roast, trimmed
1 pound fresh button mushrooms
Medium-size head Boston lettuce
Medium-size bunch celery
Small bunch red radishes
Small bunch scallions
Small bunch Italian parsley (optional)
3 cloves garlic
2 medium-size tart green apples, such as Granny Smith
½ pint heavy cream
1 stick plus 3 tablespoons unsalted butter or margarine, approximately
¼ pound Gruyère cheese
5 tablespoons olive oil
1 tablespoon vegetable oil
1 tablespoon red wine vinegar
1 tablespoon Dijon mustard
¼ cup all-purpose flour
½ pound fresh spinach noodles
4 thin slices white bread
½ teaspoon ground nutmeg
½ teaspoon paprika
Salt and freshly ground black pepper
Freshly ground white pepper
¾ cup dry white wine
2 tablespoons Madeira wine

UTENSILS

Large heavy-gauge skillet with cover
Medium-size heavy-gauge skillet or sauté pan
Large saucepan
Small saucepan or butter warmer
13 x 9-inch cookie sheet
Medium-size bowl
2 small bowls
Colander
Large plate
Salad spinner (optional)
Measuring cups and spoons
Chef's knife
Paring knife
2 wooden spoons
Slotted spoon
Small whisk
Pastry brush
Plastic or paper bag

START-TO-FINISH STEPS

1. Prepare garlic for mushrooms and salad recipes.
2. Follow mushrooms recipe steps 1 through 3.
3. Follow pork recipe steps 1 through 3.
4. Follow salad recipe steps 1 and 2.
5. Follow mushrooms recipe step 4.
6. Follow pork recipe steps 4 through 6.
7. Follow mushrooms recipe steps 5 and 6, and serve.
8. Follow pork recipe steps 7 through 9, salad recipe step 3, and serve.

RECIPES

Sautéed Button Mushrooms on Garlic Toast

1 stick unsalted butter or margarine
4 thin slices white bread
1 pound fresh button mushrooms
Medium-size head Boston lettuce
Small bunch Italian parsley for garnish (optional)
2 cloves garlic, peeled and halved
2 tablespoons olive oil
2 tablespoons Madeira wine

1. Preheat oven to 350 degrees. Melt 6 tablespoons butter in small saucepan or butter warmer over low heat. Brush both sides of bread slices with butter. Place bread on small cookie sheet and bake 12 to 15 minutes, or until golden brown.

2. Wipe mushrooms with damp paper towels and slice thinly. Wash lettuce and dry with paper towels. Divide leaves among 4 salad plates. Rinse parsley, if using, and dry. Chop enough to measure 2 tablespoons and set aside.

3. Remove toast from oven and reduce oven temperature to 200 degrees. Rub toast with cut sides of garlic cloves and cut each slice in half diagonally. Place 2 triangles on each plate.

4. In medium-size heavy-gauge skillet or sauté pan, heat olive oil with remaining 2 tablespoons butter over medium heat until foam subsides. Add mushrooms and sauté 8 to 10 minutes, or until tender but not soft.

5. Increase heat to high, add Madeira, and cook, stirring, 1 to 2 minutes, or until liquid evaporates.

6. Spoon mushrooms over toast and garnish each serving with parsley, if desired. Serve immediately.

Pork and Apples with Spinach Noodles

Small bunch scallions
1½ pounds blade Boston pork roast, trimmed
¼ cup all-purpose flour
1½ teaspoons salt
½ teaspoon paprika
½ teaspoon ground nutmeg
Pinch of freshly ground white pepper
3 tablespoons unsalted butter or margarine, approximately
1 tablespoon vegetable oil
2 medium-size tart green apples, such as Granny Smith
¾ cup dry white wine
½ cup heavy cream
½ pound fresh spinach noodles

1. Rinse scallions and dry with paper towels. Trim off ends and chop; set aside. Cut pork into ½-inch-thick strips, each about 2 inches long.

2. In plastic or paper bag, combine flour, salt, paprika, nutmeg, and pepper. Add pork and shake to coat.

3. In large skillet, melt 2 tablespoons butter with vegetable oil over medium-high heat, about 1 minute. When foam subsides, add half the pork and sauté, stirring occasionally with wooden spoon, until browned, about 8 minutes. Using slotted spoon, transfer pork to large plate. Add

remaining tablespoon butter, if required, and repeat process for remaining pork. Reserve fat in skillet.

4. Add chopped scallions to same skillet and sauté over low heat about 3 minutes, or until soft. Meanwhile, rinse and dry apples; core and cut into ½-inch-thick wedges. Transfer scallions to small bowl, cover with foil, and set aside.

5. In large saucepan, bring 2 quarts water and 1 teaspoon salt to a boil over medium-high heat. Place 4 dinner plates in 200-degree oven to warm.

6. Meanwhile, return pork and any accumulated liquid on plate to skillet. Add apple wedges, white wine, and heavy cream. Bring liquid to a boil over medium heat, cover, reduce heat to low, and simmer 20 minutes, or until pork is tender.

7. Add noodles to boiling water and cook just until tender, 4 to 5 minutes. Turn noodles into colander to drain, then return them to saucepan and heat briefly over low heat until moisture evaporates. Divide noodles among 4 warmed dinner plates.

8. Using slotted spoon, top each serving of noodles with pork and apples.

9. Increase heat under pan to high and bring juices to a boil. Cook, stirring, until sauce is thick and smooth, about 2 minutes; stir in reserved scallions. Top each serving of pork and apples with sauce, and serve.

Celery, Radish, and Gruyère Salad

6 stalks celery
¼ pound Gruyère cheese
Small bunch red radishes
3 tablespoons olive oil
1 tablespoon red wine vinegar
1 clove garlic, minced
1 tablespoon Dijon mustard
Freshly ground black pepper

1. Wash celery, dry, and cut into 2-inch lengths. Cut each length of celery into ¼-inch-thick julienne strips. Cut cheese into ¼-inch-thick by 2-inch-long julienne. Wash, trim, dry, and thinly slice radishes. In medium-size bowl, combine celery, Gruyère, and radishes.

2. In small bowl, whisk together olive oil, vinegar, minced garlic, mustard, and pepper to taste. Pour dressing over salad and toss until evenly coated; cover with plastic wrap and set aside.

3. Just before serving, toss salad to recombine and divide among dinner plates.

Avocado and Grapefruit Salad
Mexican-style Pork with Green Chilies / Warm Tortillas
Tomatoes with Cucumber Sauce

Serve this colorful Mexican-style meal on individual dinner plates or on casual ceramic platters.

The blade Boston pork roast of Menu 2, an economical cut, is cubed for the Mexican stew in this menu. (See page 9 for information on this cut.) Coriander (cilantro in Spanish markets) and chilies are necessary ingredients for an authentic Mexican flavor. Flour tortillas are called for, but the cornmeal variety will also do.

You will need two ripe avocados, so you may have to shop ahead. An unripe avocado will soften in a day or two if wrapped in a brown paper bag and left at room temperature. To test for ripeness, push a toothpick into the fruit near the stem end. Always peel and slice an avocado just before serving.

WHAT TO DRINK

A spicy, flavorful meal such as this should be accompanied by beer or ale. Dark Mexican beers or brown ales are all good choices.

SHOPPING LIST AND STAPLES

1½ pounds blade Boston pork roast, cut into ½-inch cubes
3 large ripe tomatoes (each about ¾ pound), preferably beefsteak
2 ripe avocados
Large onion (about ½ pound)
Medium-size cucumber
1 head Romaine or Boston lettuce
Small bunch fresh coriander
Small bunch fresh dill, or 2 teaspoons dried
2 cloves garlic
2 large grapefruits
Small lime
3½-ounce can green chilies, such as jalapeño (hot) or Anaheim (mild)
8-ounce container sour cream or plain low-fat yogurt
1 stick butter or margarine (optional)
2 tablespoons vegetable shortening
2 tablespoons corn oil
1 tablespoon red wine vinegar
12 to 16 fresh flour tortillas, or 1 package frozen
¼ cup sugar
5-ounce package pine nuts
1 teaspoon ground cumin
1 teaspoon dry mustard
½ teaspoon dried oregano
Salt

UTENSILS

Large Dutch oven or flameproof casserole with cover
13 x 9-inch baking sheet
2 medium-size bowls
Small bowl
2 large plates
Salad spinner (optional)
Measuring cups and spoons
Chef's knife
Paring knife
2 wooden spoons
Whisk
Melon baller (optional)

START-TO-FINISH STEPS

One hour ahead: If using frozen tortillas, set out to thaw.

Thirty minutes ahead: If using butter for tortillas, set out at room temperature.

1. Follow salad recipe steps 1 through 3.
2. Follow pork recipe steps 1 through 3.
3. While pork is browning, follow tortillas recipe step 1.
4. Follow pork recipe step 4 and tomatoes recipe step 1.
5. Follow pork recipe steps 5 and 6, and tomatoes recipe steps 2 and 3.
6. Follow pork recipe step 7 and tortillas recipe step 2.
7. Follow salad recipe steps 4 and 5, and serve as first course, if desired.
8. Follow tomatoes recipe step 4, tortillas recipe step 3, pork recipe step 8, and serve.

RECIPES

Avocado and Grapefruit Salad

1 head Romaine or Boston lettuce
2 large grapefruits
¼ cup sugar
1 tablespoon red wine vinegar
1 teaspoon dry mustard
½ teaspoon salt
2 tablespoons corn oil
2 ripe avocados

1. Wash lettuce and dry in salad spinner or with paper towels. Line salad bowl or 4 salad plates with leaves.

2. Peel grapefruits and cut into sections over small bowl to catch juice. Reserve juice; add grapefruit sections to lettuce-lined bowl or divide among plates. Cover with plastic wrap and refrigerate until ready to serve.

3. Add sugar, wine vinegar, mustard, and salt to grapefruit juice, and whisk until thoroughly blended. Add corn oil in a slow, steady stream, whisking until dressing is thick and smooth; set aside.

4. Peel avocados, halve lengthwise, and remove pits. Cut avocados crosswise into ¼- to ½-inch-thick slices and place on lettuce.

5. Whisk dressing to recombine and spoon over salad.

Mexican-style Pork with Green Chilies

Large onion (about ½ pound)
Large tomato (about ¾ pound), preferably beefsteak
Small bunch fresh coriander
2 cloves garlic
3½-ounce can green chilies, such as jalapeño (hot) or Anaheim (mild)
Small lime
2 tablespoons vegetable shortening
1½ pounds blade Boston pork roast, cut into ½-inch cubes
1 teaspoon salt
1 teaspoon ground cumin
½ teaspoon dried oregano
½ cup pine nuts

1. Peel and chop onion, reserving 1 teaspoon for cucumber sauce. Peel, halve, and coarsely chop tomato. Rinse coriander, dry with paper towels, and chop enough to measure 2 tablespoons. Peel and mince garlic. Drain chilies and chop. Squeeze enough lime to measure 2 to 3 teaspoons juice; set aside.

2. Preheat oven to 350 degrees.

3. In large Dutch oven or casserole, melt shortening over medium-high heat. Add half the pork and sauté, stirring occasionally, until browned, about 8 minutes.

4. With slotted spoon, transfer pork to plate and repeat for remaining pork. Pour off fat.

5. Return pork and accumulated juices to Dutch oven or casserole. Add onion, tomato, coriander, garlic, chilies, salt, cumin, and oregano and stir to combine. Add 1 cup water and bring to a boil over high heat. Cover, reduce heat to low, and simmer pork about 20 minutes, or until tender.

6. Meanwhile, spread pine nuts on baking sheet and toast in oven 8 to 10 minutes, or until lightly browned.

7. Remove nuts from oven and set aside. Reduce oven temperature to 200 degrees.

8. Stir lime juice into pork mixture, divide pork among 4 dinner plates or turn out onto platter, and sprinkle with pine nuts.

Warm Tortillas

12 to 16 fresh flour tortillas, or 1 package frozen, thawed
1 stick butter or margarine, at room temperature (optional)

1. Place 1 tortilla on large sheet of aluminum foil and spread evenly with about 1 teaspoon butter, if desired. Repeat, stacking tortillas on top of one another, to form 2 piles. Wrap ends of aluminum foil over stacks to enclose.

2. Place foil-wrapped tortillas in 200-degree oven for 10 to 15 minutes.

3. Just before serving, remove tortillas from oven and unwrap. Roll 4 tortillas and place 1 roll, seam-side down, on each dinner plate. Place remaining tortillas in napkin-lined basket and serve separately.

Tomatoes with Cucumber Sauce

2 large ripe tomatoes (each about ¾ pound), preferably beefsteak
Medium-size cucumber
Small bunch fresh dill, or 2 teaspoons dried
1 cup sour cream or plain low-fat yogurt
1 teaspoon chopped onion, reserved from pork recipe
¼ teaspoon salt

1. Rinse tomatoes and dry with paper towels. Core and cut tomatoes into ½-inch-thick slices and divide slices among dinner plates.

2. Rinse cucumber and fresh dill, if using. Halve cucumber lengthwise. With teaspoon or melon baller, remove seeds, then dice. Chop enough dill to measure 2 tablespoons and reserve 8 sprigs for garnish, if desired.

3. In medium-size bowl, combine cucumber, dill, sour cream, onion, and salt, and stir until well blended; set aside.

4. Just before serving, spoon sauce over tomato slices and garnish with dill sprigs, if desired.

Leon, Stanley, and Evan Lobel

MENU 1 (Right)
Pork Chops Braised with Onions
Oven-Fried Potato Wedges
Baked Tomatoes

MENU 2
Pork Scallopini
Linguine with Garlic, Onions, and Zucchini
Asparagus with Lemon Butter

MENU 3
Ham-and-Rice-Stuffed Peppers
Broccoli and Carrots with Pine Nuts
Tossed Salad with Garlic-Mustard Dressing

Selling and promoting quality meats and meat products is a full-time job for the Lobel family. But even in their leisure hours, they enjoy experimenting with new recipes for meats—including various cuts of pork. According to these experts, "Today's tender, disease-free pork lends itself to cooking techniques such as sautéing, and people no longer need think twice about grinding the meat for patties or having it cubed for kebabs."

In Menu 1, the cooks use boned pork chops, but instead of pan frying them for a long period of time, they brown the chops to enhance their appearance and flavor and then braise them with slices of onion. Oven-fried potato wedges and lightly stuffed baked tomatoes accompany the pork.

To further demonstrate the versatility of pork, in Menu 2 the Lobels pound boneless slices cut from the tenderloin into very thin scallops. These scallops, like their tender veal counterparts, are ideal for quick cooking. Here they are sautéed and topped with a lemon sauce.

For the busy cook, Menu 3 combines diced ham steak with rice and seasonings as a filling for green bell peppers. With the peppers, the Lobels serve fresh broccoli and carrots with pine nuts and a tossed salad with garlic-mustard dressing.

For a family-style meal, serve the pork chops braised with onion slices and the baked tomatoes on large platters, and put the crisp potato wedges in a napkin-lined wooden bowl.

Pork Chops Braised with Onions
Oven-Fried Potato Wedges
Baked Tomatoes

The pork chops should fit comfortably in a pan without overlapping so they cook in the flavorful stock. If your skillet is very large or has a high, domed cover, place a sheet of aluminum foil over the chops before covering the pan (pierce the foil with a pin to allow steam to escape). Braising the pork chops allows the garlic, onion, and herb flavors to permeate the meat and produces a rich sauce that needs no further reduction.

A curved grapefruit knife or serrated grapefruit spoon is useful for removing the seeds from the tomatoes, but do not remove all the pulp.

A quick way to peel the garlic cloves for the pork recipe is to lay them on a cutting board and press with the flat of a heavy knife until the skins pop. You can then easily remove the skins with your fingers.

WHAT TO DRINK

The straightforward flavors of these dishes will be complemented by either a reasonably firm white Mâcon or a delicate German Riesling.

SHOPPING LIST AND STAPLES

Four 1-inch-thick rib pork chops (each about ½ pound), backbone removed and trimmed of fat
4 large tomatoes (about 3 pounds total weight)
4 large Idaho potatoes (about 2¼ pounds total weight)
3 medium-size onions (about 1 pound total weight)
1 head garlic
Small bunch fresh basil or oregano, or 1 tablespoon dried
Small bunch fresh parsley
Small bunch fresh thyme or oregano, or 1 teaspoon dried
1 tablespoon unsalted butter
2 ounces Parmesan cheese
1 cup chicken or vegetable stock, preferably homemade (see page 13), or canned
¾ cup vegetable oil, approximately
½ cup all-purpose flour
1 slice home-style white bread
Dash of paprika (optional)
Salt
Freshly ground pepper

UTENSILS

Food processor or blender
Large skillet with cover
13 x 9-inch baking pan
Small baking pan or dish
9-inch pie pan or shallow dish
Small bowl
Measuring cups and spoons
Chef's knife
Slotted spoon
Wooden spoon
Spatula
Grater
Pastry brush
Metal tongs

START-TO-FINISH STEPS

1. Follow potatoes recipe steps 1 through 3.
2. Follow pork chops recipe steps 1 through 5.
3. Follow tomatoes recipe steps 1 through 3.
4. About 10 minutes before chops are finished, follow tomatoes recipe step 4.
5. Follow pork chops recipe step 6, potatoes recipe step 4, and tomatoes recipe step 5, and serve while hot.

RECIPES

Pork Chops Braised with Onions

3 medium-size onions (about 1 pound total weight)
6 to 8 cloves garlic
Small bunch fresh thyme or oregano, or 1 teaspoon dried
½ cup vegetable oil
Four 1-inch-thick rib pork chops (each about ½ pound), backbone removed and trimmed of fat
Salt
Freshly ground pepper
½ cup all-purpose flour
1 cup chicken or vegetable stock

1. Peel onions and cut into ¼-inch-thick slices. Peel 6 to 8 garlic cloves, according to taste, and slice thinly. Rinse thyme, dry with paper towels, and chop enough to measure 1 tablespoon. Reserve remaining thyme for another use.

2. In large skillet, warm ¼ cup of the oil over medium heat. Add onions and sauté 6 to 10 minutes, or until translucent; remove from pan with slotted spoon and set aside.
3. Meanwhile, season chops with salt and pepper to taste. In pie pan or shallow dish, combine flour and chopped thyme. Dredge chops in flour mixture, shaking off excess.
4. Add remaining oil to skillet and increase heat to medium-high. When oil is hot, add chops, arranging in single layer, and sear 1 to 2 minutes per side to seal in juices. Then sauté chops until golden brown, 3 to 4 minutes; turn chops, add sliced garlic to pan, and sauté second side 3 to 5 minutes, until golden. Stir garlic slices to brown them.
5. Add stock and reserved onions to skillet. Cover, reduce heat to low, and braise chops 30 to 40 minutes, until tender and cooked through.
6. Transfer pork chops to platter, top with onions and pan sauce, and serve hot.

Oven-Fried Potato Wedges

4 large Idaho potatoes (about 2¼ pounds total
    weight)
2 tablespoons vegetable oil, approximately
Salt
Freshly ground pepper
Dash of paprika (optional)

1. Preheat oven to 400 degrees.
2. Scrub potatoes under running water and dry. Slice each potato lengthwise into 8 wedges. Place wedges on plate, brush with oil, and season with salt, pepper, and paprika to taste. Arrange potatoes in single layer in large baking pan.
3. Place potato wedges in oven and bake 30 to 45 minutes, or until crisp.
4. Transfer potatoes to napkin-lined bowl and serve hot.

Baked Tomatoes

4 large tomatoes (about 3 pounds total weight)
Small bunch fresh parsley
Small bunch fresh basil or oregano, or 1 tablespoon
    dried
2 cloves garlic
1 slice home-style white bread
Freshly ground pepper
1 tablespoon vegetable oil
2 ounces Parmesan cheese
1 tablespoon unsalted butter

1. Cut off tops of tomatoes, remove seeds, leaving most of pulp intact, and set aside to drain, upside down. Rinse parsley and basil, and dry with paper towels. Chop enough parsley to measure 2 teaspoons and enough basil for 2 tablespoons. Reserve remaining herbs for another use. Peel garlic and mince. Using food processor or blender, make enough bread crumbs to measure about ¼ cup.
2. In small bowl, combine bread crumbs, parsley, basil,

garlic, and pepper to taste. Stir in oil. Spoon crumb mixture evenly into tomatoes.
3. Grate Parmesan. Place tomatoes in small baking pan and top filling with a sprinkling of Parmesan. Set tomatoes aside until ready to bake.
4. Cut butter into small pieces and dot on top of tomatoes. Place tomatoes in 400-degree oven and bake about 10 minutes, or until tops are lightly browned and skins are slightly crinkled.
5. Remove tomatoes from oven, transfer to platter, and serve.

ADDED TOUCH

If you cannot find maple sugar to sweeten this rich custard, use the same amount of pure maple syrup.

Mocha Bavarian Cream

3 egg yolks
3 tablespoons plus ¼ teaspoon maple sugar or maple
    syrup
1 teaspoon vanilla extract
2 cups milk
1 tablespoon instant coffee powder
1 teaspoon unsweetened cocoa powder
1 tablespoon unflavored gelatin
1 cup heavy cream

1. Lightly oil a 1-quart mold or serving bowl.
2. In medium-size bowl, using electric mixer, beat egg yolks with maple sugar until thick and creamy, about 2 minutes. Stir in vanilla.
3. In medium-size heavy-gauge saucepan, scald milk over low heat. Remove pan from heat, add instant coffee and cocoa, and stir until dissolved, 4 to 5 minutes.
4. Beating constantly, pour milk mixture very slowly into egg mixture, until well blended.
5. Pour egg-milk mixture into saucepan and cook, stirring, over low heat until custard coats back of wooden spoon, 3 to 4 minutes. Pour custard through strainer into metal bowl and set aside to cool.
6. Place ¼ cup water in small bowl and sprinkle gelatin on top; let stand 5 minutes. Place bowl in pan of hot water, stirring gelatin occasionally until dissolved, about 5 minutes.
7. Pour dissolved gelatin into custard and stir to blend. Place bowl of custard mixture in larger bowl filled with ice cubes and stir until custard starts to thicken, about 5 minutes.
8. In mixing bowl, whip heavy cream with electric mixer set at high speed until it holds a soft shape. With rubber spatula, stir in ¼ teaspoon maple sugar. Reserve half the whipped cream in separate bowl; cover with plastic wrap and place in refrigerator until needed. Gently fold remaining whipped cream into custard. Turn mixture into mold and refrigerate to chill until firm, about 2 hours.
9. When ready to serve, gently run wet knife around edge of mold, invert mold on platter, and gently shake to release cream. Top Bavarian cream with reserved whipped cream.

Pork Scallopini
Linguine with Garlic, Onions, and Zucchini
Asparagus with Lemon Butter

Select bright green asparagus spears that are straight and have compact tips. Open leafy tips are sure signs of age. Avoid any that are withered or soft or that have woody white bases. Thick spears will often be more tender than those that are pencil thin. To store asparagus for a few days, cut off a small piece from the bottom of each stem, place upright in an inch of water, and refrigerate. The asparagus should stay fresh for several days. Do not overcook the spears—asparagus should be crunchy.

Pork scallopini garnished with lemon slices and individual bundles of asparagus make a light springtime dinner. The linguine with zucchini, garlic, and onions can be prepared and served as a first course.

WHAT TO DRINK

For a white wine, choose Italian Greco di Tufo or Cortese di Gavi. For red, select an inexpensive California Merlot or a shipper's Saint-Émilion.

SHOPPING LIST AND STAPLES

4 pork scallops, cut from eye of loin (about 2 pounds total weight), pounded to ⅛ inch thick
1½ pounds asparagus (16 to 20 spears)
2 medium-size zucchini (about ¾ pound)
2 medium-size onions (about ¾ pound)
1 head garlic
Small bunch basil

Small bunch dill for garnish (optional)
Small bunch parsley for garnish (optional)
Small bunch thyme or oregano for garnish (optional)
4 medium-size lemons
6 tablespoons unsalted butter
¼ pound Parmesan cheese
½ cup plus 1 tablespoon vegetable oil
½ cup all-purpose flour
¾ pound fresh or dried linguine
Salt and freshly ground pepper

UTENSILS

Stockpot or large kettle
2 large skillets
Small saucepan
Vegetable steamer
Ovenproof dish
Pie pan or shallow dish
Colander
Measuring cups and spoons
Chef's knife
Paring knife
2 wooden spoons
Grater
Juicer

Metal tongs
Vegetable peeler
Kitchen string

START-TO-FINISH STEPS

1. Rinse basil and other fresh herbs, if using, dry with paper towels, and prepare. Thinly slice 2 lemons and juice remaining 2 lemons.
2. Follow asparagus recipe step 1.
3. Follow scallopini recipe steps 1 and 2.
4. Follow linguine recipe steps 1 through 4.
5. Follow scallopini recipe step 3.
6. Follow asparagus recipe step 2 and linguine recipe step 5.
7. Follow asparagus recipe steps 3 and 4.
8. Follow linguine recipe step 6, scallopini recipe steps 4 and 5, and serve.

RECIPES

Pork Scallopini

4 pork scallops, cut from eye of loin (about 2 pounds total weight), pounded to ⅛-inch thick
½ cup all-purpose flour
Salt (optional)

Freshly ground pepper
3 tablespoons unsalted butter
¼ cup vegetable oil
2 medium-size lemons, thinly sliced, plus 2 tablespoons
  fresh lemon juice
1 tablespoon chopped thyme or oregano for garnish
  (optional)

1. Preheat oven to 200 degrees. Place 4 dinner plates in oven to warm.
2. Dry meat with paper towels. Place flour in pie pan or shallow dish. Place scallops in flour and dredge lightly, shaking off excess. Season each scallop with salt and pepper to taste, and set aside.
3. In large skillet, melt 2 tablespoons butter with vegetable oil over medium-high heat. When fat is hot, add scallops and sauté quickly 2 minutes. Using tongs, turn scallops and cook another 2 minutes, or until lightly browned. Place 1 scallop on each warmed plate and return to oven (no longer than 15 minutes or scallops will dry out).
4. Meanwhile, add lemon juice to skillet. Over medium heat, using wooden spoon, scrape up any brown bits clinging to pan. Add pepper to taste. Add remaining tablespoon of butter, stirring until it melts and thickens sauce, about 2 to 3 minutes.
5. Remove scallops from oven. Spoon butter sauce on each and sprinkle with chopped thyme, if desired. Garnish scallops with lemon slices, and serve.

Linguine with Garlic, Onions, and Zucchini

¼ cup plus 1 tablespoon vegetable oil
1 tablespoon salt
2 medium-size onions (about ¾ pound)
2 medium-size zucchini (about ¾ pound)
8 cloves garlic
¼ pound Parmesan cheese
⅓ cup chopped fresh basil
Freshly ground pepper
¾ pound fresh or dried linguine
1 tablespoon unsalted butter
1 tablespoon chopped fresh parsley for garnish (optional)

1. In stockpot or large kettle, bring water to a boil, with 1 tablespoon vegetable oil and salt, for linguine. Place serving dish in oven to warm.
2. Peel and cut onions into thin slices; separate into rings. Rinse zucchini, dry, and cut into ½-inch-thick dice. Peel

and chop garlic. Grate enough Parmesan to measure ½ to ¾ cup.
3. In large skillet, heat ¼ cup oil over medium-high heat. Add onions and sauté 2 to 3 minutes, stirring. Add garlic and zucchini and sauté, stirring, 3 to 5 minutes.
4. Stir in chopped basil and pepper to taste, turn into ovenproof dish, and keep warm in 200-degree oven.
5. Slowly add linguine to boiling water and cook 4 to 5 minutes for fresh or 8 to 12 minutes for dried, or until *al dente*. Turn pasta into colander to drain; dry stockpot.
6. Return pasta to stockpot over medium heat, stir in butter, and toss until melted. Transfer linguine to warm serving dish, spoon zucchini mixture over top, sprinkle with Parmesan, and chopped parsley, if desired.

Asparagus with Lemon Butter

1½ pounds asparagus (16 to 20 spears)
2 tablespoons unsalted butter
1 to 2 tablespoons fresh lemon juice
4 dill sprigs for garnish (optional)

1. Trim and peel asparagus stems (see illustration). Tie spears with kitchen string into 4 equal bundles.
2. In medium-size saucepan fitted with vegetable steamer, bring ½ inch water to a gentle boil over medium heat. Add asparagus and steam 5 to 7 minutes, or until tender when pierced with tip of a knife.
3. Meanwhile, in small saucepan, melt butter over medium heat, add lemon juice, and stir until sauce thickens, 2 to 3 minutes.
4. Drain asparagus in colander. Divide bundles among dinner plates, top with lemon butter and dill sprigs, if desired, and keep warm in 200-degree oven until ready to serve.

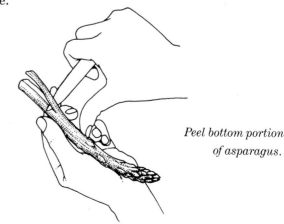

*Peel bottom portion
of asparagus.*

Ham-and-Rice-Stuffed Peppers
Broccoli and Carrots with Pine Nuts
Tossed Salad with Garlic-Mustard Dressing

Steamed broccoli and carrots with pine nuts complement the green bell peppers stuffed with a mixture of ham, rice, and cheese. Offer some grated Parmesan for sprinkling over the tossed salad.

The best peppers for stuffing are those with thick skins and even bottoms (so they don't topple over while baking). Be sure to remove all of the seeds because they are often bitter. Steaming the peppers before stuffing partially tenderizes them and cuts down on the baking time.

Alfalfa sprouts and *daikon* (a white Japanese radish) are used in the salad. Be sure to keep the sprouts refrigerated until needed; they deteriorate rapidly. Long and slender, a *daikon* is shaped like a large white carrot and has a sharp but sweet flavor. Select a firm *daikon* with dark green leaves and store it in the refrigerator tightly wrapped in plastic. Oriental groceries or supermarkets stocking exotic produce sell these radishes.

WHAT TO DRINK

Try a red wine such as California Gamay Beaujolais, Chianti Classico, or Saint-Émilion with this simple dinner.

SHOPPING LIST AND STAPLES

¾-pound ham steak
Medium-size bunch broccoli (about 1 pound)
4 very large green bell peppers (about 1¾ pounds total weight)
Small red bell pepper
Medium-size seedless cucumber, or 2 small thin zucchini
Medium-size daikon (about ½ pound), or 1 bunch red or white radishes
2 medium-size onions (about 1 pound total weight)
4 medium-size carrots (about 1 pound total weight)
Medium-size head red leaf lettuce
Small bunch alfalfa sprouts
4 medium-size mushrooms (optional)
Small bunch fresh parsley
Small bunch fresh basil, or 1 teaspoon dried
Small bunch fresh oregano, or ½ teaspoon dried
Small bunch fresh thyme, or ½ teaspoon dried
1 head garlic

91

Large lemon
4 tablespoons unsalted butter
½ pound mozzarella cheese
2 ounces Parmesan cheese
2 cups chicken stock, preferably homemade (see page 13), or canned
1 cup safflower oil
3 tablespoons vegetable oil
1 tablespoon Dijon mustard
1 cup long-grain rice
3 tablespoons pine nuts
2-ounce package sunflower seeds
Cayenne pepper
Salt
Freshly ground pepper

UTENSILS

Food processor or blender
Medium-size skillet
Small skillet
Large saucepan with cover
Medium-size saucepan with cover
Vegetable steamer
9 x 9-inch baking pan or dish
Large bowl
Small bowl (optional)
Salad spinner (optional)
Medium-size strainer
Measuring cups and spoons
Chef's knife
Paring knife
2 wooden spoons
Spatula
Whisk (optional)
Vegetable peeler
Grater
Juicer

START-TO-FINISH STEPS

1. Follow peppers recipe steps 1 through 10.
2. Follow broccoli recipe step 1 and salad recipe steps 1 through 4.
3. Follow peppers recipe step 11.
4. Follow broccoli recipe steps 2 and 3.
5. Follow peppers recipe step 12 and broccoli recipe step 4.

6. Follow salad recipe step 5, peppers recipe step 13, broccoli recipe step 5, and serve.

RECIPES

Ham-and-Rice-Stuffed Peppers

4 very large green bell peppers (about 1¾ pounds total weight)
4 medium-size mushrooms (optional)
3 tablespoons vegetable oil
1 cup long-grain rice
2 cups chicken stock
Small bunch fresh parsley
Small bunch fresh basil, or 1 teaspoon dried
2 medium-size onions (about 1 pound total weight)
4 cloves garlic
½ pound mozzarella cheese
¾-pound ham steak
Pinch of Cayenne pepper
Salt
Freshly ground pepper
8 strips red bell pepper for garnish, reserved from salad recipe (optional)

1. Rinse green bell peppers and dry. Slice off tops of peppers, chop, and set aside. Remove membranes and seeds from whole peppers and set aside. If using mushrooms, wipe clean with damp paper towels, chop, and set aside.
2. In medium-size saucepan, heat 1 tablespoon vegetable oil over medium-high heat. Add rice and sauté, stirring, about 5 minutes, or until well coated.
3. Stir in chicken stock, and bring to a boil. Reduce heat to very low, cover pan, and simmer rice about 15 minutes, or until liquid is absorbed and rice is tender.
4. Meanwhile, preheat oven to 400 degrees. In large saucepan fitted with vegetable steamer, bring ½ inch water to a boil over medium heat. Add whole peppers and steam 5 minutes.
5. While peppers are steaming, rinse parsley and basil, and dry with paper towels. Reserve 4 parsley sprigs for garnish, if desired; chop enough of remainder to measure 2 tablespoons. Chop enough basil to measure 1 tablespoon. Reserve remaining fresh herbs for another use. Peel and chop onions; peel and mince garlic.
6. Remove peppers from steamer and drain upside down on paper towels. Grease baking pan or dish.

7. Cut 4 thin slices from mozzarella cheese and reserve; dice remainder. Cut ham steak into ¼-inch dice.

8. In medium-size skillet, heat remaining 2 tablespoons oil over medium heat. Add onions and sauté 2 to 4 minutes, or until translucent. Add minced garlic and chopped pepper tops, and sauté, stirring, 3 to 4 minutes. Add chopped mushrooms, if using, and cook another 2 minutes. Turn onion mixture into large bowl.

9. Remove rice from heat. Add diced ham and 2 cups hot rice to onion mixture, stirring to combine. Add chopped parsley, reserving about 1 teaspoon for peppers garnish, if desired. Add basil, diced cheese, a pinch of Cayenne, and salt and pepper to taste. Mix together thoroughly.

10. Divide stuffing mixture among peppers. Transfer peppers to baking pan and bake 20 minutes.

11. Top each stuffed pepper with 1 slice mozzarella and bake another 7 to 8 minutes, or until cheese melts.

12. Turn oven temperature to broil. Place peppers under broiler 4 to 6 inches from heating element for 2 to 3 minutes, or until cheese is lightly browned and bubbly.

13. With spatula, transfer 1 pepper to each dinner plate and sprinkle with reserved parsley, if using. If desired, garnish each plate with 2 strips of red bell pepper and 1 parsley sprig, and serve.

Broccoli and Carrots with Pine Nuts

Medium-size bunch broccoli (about 1 pound)
4 medium-size carrots (about 1 pound total weight)
4 tablespoons unsalted butter
3 tablespoons pine nuts
Salt and freshly ground pepper

1. Wash broccoli; trim and peel off outer layer of stems. Separate into florets. Trim carrots, scrape, and cut diagonally into ⅓-inch-thick slices.

2. In medium-size saucepan fitted with vegetable steamer, bring about ½ inch water to a boil over medium heat. Place broccoli and carrots in steamer, cover, and steam 5 to 8 minutes, or until crisp-tender when pierced with point of knife.

3. Meanwhile, melt butter in small skillet over medium-high heat. Add pine nuts and sauté until lightly golden, about 3 to 4 minutes. Remove pan from heat.

4. Remove steamer from heat when vegetables are done and season them with salt and pepper to taste.

5. Divide vegetables among 4 dinner plates and top each serving with sautéed pine nuts.

Tossed Salad with Garlic-Mustard Dressing

2 ounces Parmesan cheese
Medium-size head red leaf lettuce
Small bunch fresh oregano, or ½ teaspoon dried
Small bunch fresh thyme, or ½ teaspoon dried
Large lemon
3 cloves garlic
1 tablespoon Dijon mustard
Pinch of Cayenne pepper
Freshly ground pepper
1 cup safflower oil
Small bunch alfalfa sprouts
Medium-size seedless cucumber, or 2 small thin zucchini
Medium-size daikon (about ½ pound), or 1 bunch red or white radishes
Small red bell pepper
¼ cup sunflower seeds

1. Grate enough Parmesan to measure ¼ cup and place in small serving bowl. Wash lettuce and dry in salad spinner or with paper towels. Tear into bite-size pieces and place in large bowl. Rinse oregano and thyme, dry with paper towels, and chop enough of each to measure 1 teaspoon, reserving remainder for another use. Squeeze enough lemon juice to measure 3 tablespoons. Peel garlic.

2. For dressing, place garlic in food processor fitted with steel blade and mince finely, or mince with chef's knife and place in small bowl. Add lemon juice, mustard, oregano, thyme, Cayenne pepper, and freshly ground pepper to taste. With machine running if using processor, or whisking continuously, add oil in a slow, steady stream and process or whisk until well blended. If dressing is too thick, add water, 1 tablespoon at a time, blending after each addition until desired consistency is reached.

3. Place sprouts in medium-size strainer, rinse, and drain. Wash cucumber, daikon, and red bell pepper. Thinly slice cucumber and add to lettuce. Peel daikon, cut into thin strips, and add to lettuce. Halve, core, and remove seeds and membranes from pepper. Cut into ½-inch-thick strips, reserving 8 strips to garnish dinner plates, if desired. Add bell pepper to salad and sprinkle with sunflower seeds.

4. Process or whisk dressing to recombine and pour over salad. Toss, cover bowl with plastic wrap, and refrigerate until ready to serve.

5. Divide salad among 4 small plates and serve Parmesan separately.

Alice Ross

Because she owns an extensive collection of antique kitchen utensils and cookbooks, food scholar Alice Ross can faithfully re-create meals from bygone eras. She likes to adapt old-time recipes to contemporary tastes, cookware, and ingredients without losing the appeal of the original meal. For example, her Menu 3—sausage-stuffed pork rolls, Dutch oven cornbread, and a salad of wild greens—is a meal that our early American ancestors might well have prepared. The sausage seasonings are the same as those used in the eighteenth century, and although the moist cornbread would originally have baked in a pile of embers on the hearth, it is just as good when baked in a modern oven. The salad resembles the "rough" salads of colonial days; its creamy vinaigrette dressing is inspired by an American recipe of 1833.

In Menu 1, Alice Ross presents a classic southern dinner of country ham and biscuits but gives it a modern twist by adding mild goat cheese to the dough. The red cabbage salad is a variation on traditional cole slaw.

Menu 2, which reflects the cook's interest in ethnic cuisines, is a typical peasant meal from Spain. Richly flavored ham and smoked garlic-flavored sausages are combined with shellfish, red bell pepper, and onion in a hearty stew that is served over saffron rice.

Goat cheese biscuits bake—and are served—on top of country ham for this hearty "down home" meal. Present the red cabbage slaw on a kale-lined platter for the best visual effect.

Country Ham Steak in Creamy Mustard Sauce
Flaky Goat Cheese Biscuits
Red Cabbage Slaw

At one time the primary sweetener in this country, molasses is still used in many regional dishes, such as this ham steak recipe from the South. The cook calls for mild Barbados molasses, made from sugar cane, which is available at many health food stores. You can substitute any mild molasses, but not blackstrap molasses, which is too strong for this dish.

Select a young, mild domestic goat cheese (chèvre) for the biscuits. It is generally less salty than the imported types and will be more compatible with the country ham. You can use feta, drained of its brine and rinsed well, or farmer cheese instead.

WHAT TO DRINK

A firm, full-bodied white wine would complement this tasty dinner. The cook suggests a good American Chardonnay or a French Meursault.

SHOPPING LIST AND STAPLES

1½-inch-thick ham steak, cut from center of precooked country ham (about 1¾ pounds)
Small bunch kale
Small head red cabbage (about 1 pound)
1 to 2 cloves garlic (optional)
½ cup plus 1 tablespoon milk
1 quart half-and-half or light cream, approximately
1 stick unsalted butter, approximately
¼ pound domestic goat cheese
½ cup olive oil
2 tablespoons red or white wine vinegar
1 tablespoon whole-grain mustard
2 to 3 drops Worcestershire sauce
2 tablespoons mild molasses, preferably Barbados
1 tablespoon honey
2 cups flour, preferably unbleached
1 tablespoon plus 1 teaspoon baking powder
½ teaspoon dry mustard
Salt and freshly ground black pepper

UTENSILS

Food processor (optional)
Shallow casserole or baking dish
15 x 10-inch baking sheet
2 large serving platters

2 large bowls
Small bowl
Salad spinner (optional)
Measuring cups and spoons
Chef's knife
Paring knife
Wooden spoon
2 large spatulas
Whisk
Pastry blender (optional)

START-TO-FINISH STEPS

1. Follow ham recipe steps 1 through 3.
2. Follow biscuits recipe steps 1 through 4.
3. Follow ham recipe steps 4 and 5.
4. While biscuits are baking, follow slaw recipe steps 1 through 5 and ham recipe step 6.
5. Follow ham recipe step 7 and serve with biscuits and slaw.

RECIPES

Country Ham Steak in Creamy Mustard Sauce

1½-inch-thick ham steak, cut from center of precooked country ham (about 1¾ pounds)
1 tablespoon whole-grain mustard
2 tablespoons mild molasses, preferably Barbados
2 to 3 cups half-and-half or light cream
Dough for Flaky Goat Cheese Biscuits (see following recipe)

1. Preheat oven to 350 degrees.
2. Rub both sides of ham steak with mustard and place in shallow casserole or baking dish just large enough to contain it. Drizzle molasses over ham.
3. Pour in just enough half-and-half or cream to reach up to but not cover the top of ham and bake 25 minutes.
4. Using two large spatulas, turn steak over. Increase oven temperature to 425 degrees.
5. Using about two tablespoons dough for each biscuit, drop dough onto ham until it is completely covered. Drop remaining dough onto greased baking sheet. Bake until biscuits are crusty and golden, 25 minutes.
6. Place platter under hot running water to warm.
7. Dry platter. Carefully transfer ham and biscuits to platter and surround with pan juices.

Flaky Goat Cheese Biscuits

2 cups flour, preferably unbleached
1 tablespoon plus 1 teaspoon baking powder
1 stick unsalted butter, plus additional butter for greasing
¼ pound domestic goat cheese
½ cup plus 1 tablespoon milk
¼ cup half-and-half or light cream

1. In large bowl, combine flour and baking powder and stir with fork to mix. Using pastry blender or two knives, cut in butter until it is the size of peas.
2. Crumble goat cheese and stir into flour mixture.
3. Grease baking sheet; set aside.
4. Add milk and half-and-half or cream and stir just until moistened; set aside. (See step 5 for ham steak.)

Red Cabbage Slaw

Small bunch kale
Small head red cabbage (about 1 pound)
1 to 2 cloves garlic (optional)
½ cup olive oil
2 tablespoons red or white wine vinegar
½ teaspoon dry mustard
2 to 3 drops Worcestershire sauce
1 tablespoon honey
Salt and freshly ground black pepper

1. Wash kale and dry in salad spinner or with paper towels. Discard any battered or discolored leaves. Trim off tough stems and discard. Arrange 6 to 8 leaves on serving platter; refrigerate remainder for another use.
2. Remove tough or blemished outer leaves from cabbage and discard. Core and quarter cabbage. Using food processor with shredding disk, or chef's knife, shred cabbage. Turn cabbage into large bowl and set aside.
3. If using garlic, peel and mince.
4. In small bowl, combine garlic, olive oil, vinegar, mustard, Worcestershire sauce, honey, and salt and pepper to taste, and whisk until blended. Set aside.
5. Pour dressing over cabbage and toss to coat thoroughly. Mound cabbage on top of bed of kale.

ADDED TOUCH

Bosc pears with chocolate sauce are a refreshing conclusion to a hearty meal. Anjou or Bartlett pears may also be used for this recipe.

Cold Gingered Pears with Hot Chocolate Sauce

4 Bosc pears with stems attached (about 1 pound total weight)
1 lemon
¾ cup ginger ale
2 tablespoons sugar
2 tablespoons pear liqueur (optional)
Hot Chocolate Sauce (see following recipe)
6 slices candied ginger for garnish, slivered (optional)

1. Preheat oven to 400 degrees.
2. Wash pears and stand them close together in an ovenproof loaf pan.
3. Squeeze juice from half of lemon. Add juice, ginger ale, and sugar to pan; bake, basting pears 2 or 3 times, about 40 minutes, until almost tender but still firm.
4. Set pears aside to cool in pan, about 20 minutes. Add pear liqueur, if desired. Cover pan and refrigerate overnight, or at least 4 hours before serving.
5. Divide among individual plates. Top each serving with hot chocolate sauce, garnish with slivers of candied ginger, if desired, and serve.

Hot Chocolate Sauce

½ pound top-quality bittersweet chocolate
4 eggs
½ cup heavy cream
2 to 3 tablespoons chocolate liqueur, such as Sabra
2 tablespoons light corn syrup

1. Melt chocolate in top of double boiler over, not in, hot but not simmering water.
2. While chocolate is melting, separate eggs, placing yolks in small bowl and reserving whites for another use. Add heavy cream to yolks and whisk until just blended.
3. One tablespoon at a time, add melted chocolate to egg mixture, beating vigorously after each addition to prevent coagulation of eggs. After about 4 additions, quickly beat egg mixture into remaining melted chocolate. Place mixture over hot water and cook, stirring, until thick, 2 to 3 minutes.
4. Stir in liqueur and corn syrup, and taste for sweetness. Add additional corn syrup, if desired.
5. Serve immediately as a hot topping, or cool, cover, and refrigerate until ready to use. This sauce may be reheated easily in a double boiler.

Ham and Sausage Casserole with Shellfish
Saffron Rice
Wilted Spinach with Pine Nuts

For this Spanish-style meal, serve a casserole of ham, sausage, and shellfish with saffron rice and wilted spinach.

Depending on availability, you can use any combination of the shellfish listed here. Shellfish is among the most perishable of foods, so be sure to buy the clams and mussels for the casserole as close to preparation time as possible. Refrigerate them promptly and do not clean until just before cooking. Fresh shellfish have tightly closed shells. Any open shells should snap shut when tapped; discard any that remain open.

WHAT TO DRINK

An appropriate choice for this dinner would be a Spanish Rioja, either red or white. Or try a young red Italian Chianti or a California Pinot Blanc.

SHOPPING LIST AND STAPLES

½ pound linguiça or any smoked, garlic-flavored sausage, such as kielbasa or chorizo
½ pound unsliced richly flavored ham, such as Serrano, Smithfield, or prosciutto
2 dozen small steamer clams
1 dozen tiny littleneck clams
1 dozen small mussels
2 pounds spinach, approximately
6 plum tomatoes (about ¾ pound total weight), or 16-ounce can plum tomatoes
Large red bell pepper
3 medium-size onions (about 1½ pounds total weight)
3 medium-size cloves garlic
Small bunch parsley
1 lemon
1¾ cups chicken stock, preferably homemade (see page 13), or canned
¼ cup plus 3 tablespoons virgin olive oil
1 tablespoon sherry vinegar or white wine vinegar
1 cup long-grain rice
2-ounce jar pine nuts
2 bay leaves
½ teaspoon saffron threads, or ⅛ teaspoon powdered saffron
½ teaspoon Cayenne pepper, approximately
1 tablespoon paprika
Ground nutmeg
Salt and freshly ground black pepper
1 cup dry red wine, approximately

UTENSILS

Large heavy-gauge casserole or Dutch oven with cover
Medium-size heavy-gauge casserole or saucepan with cover
Large saucepan
Medium-size heavy-gauge saucepan
Large bowl
Colander
Measuring cups and spoons
Chef's knife
Paring knife
2 wooden spoons
Stiff scrub brush

START-TO-FINISH STEPS

One hour ahead: Combine clams and mussels in large bowl, cover with cold salt water, and set aside.

1. Rinse lemon and halve. Squeeze juice of one half for casserole recipe and grate zest of remaining half for spinach recipe. Follow casserole recipe steps 1 through 3.
2. While sausage is sautéing, follow rice recipe steps 1 and 2.
3. Follow casserole recipe step 4 and rice recipe step 3.
4. Follow casserole recipe steps 5 and 6.
5. While tomatoes are simmering and liquid is reducing, follow spinach recipe steps 1 and 2.
6. Follow casserole recipe step 7.
7. While shellfish is cooking, follow spinach recipe steps 3 and 4, and rice recipe step 4.
8. Follow spinach recipe step 5, casserole recipe step 8, and serve with rice.

RECIPES

Ham and Sausage Casserole with Shellfish

½ pound linguiça or any smoked, garlic-flavored sausage, such as kielbasa or chorizo
½ pound unsliced richly flavored ham, such as Serrano, Smithfield, or prosciutto
3 medium-size cloves garlic
3 medium-size onions (about 1½ pounds total weight)
Large red bell pepper
6 plum tomatoes (about ¾ pound total weight) or 16-ounce can plum tomatoes
Small bunch parsley
2 dozen small steamer clams
1 dozen tiny littleneck clams
1 dozen small mussels
3 tablespoons virgin olive oil
2 bay leaves
1 tablespoon paprika
½ teaspoon Cayenne pepper, approximately
1 teaspoon lemon juice
Freshly ground black pepper
1 cup dry red wine, approximately

1. Remove casing from sausage. Cut sausage and ham into ½-inch chunks. Peel garlic and onions. Mince garlic and cut onions into ½-inch-thick slices. Wash red bell pepper and dry. Halve, core, and seed pepper; cut into ¼-inch-thick strips. Coarsely chop tomatoes. Wash parsley and dry with paper towels. Chop parsley stems and mince leaves separately to measure about 2 tablespoons.
2. Scrub clams and mussels with stiff brush and rinse well. Discard any that have opened. Remove beards from mussels and scrape shells to remove encrustations.

3. Heat olive oil in large heavy-gauge casserole or Dutch oven over medium heat. Add sausage and ham, and sauté over medium-high heat 3 to 4 minutes, or until lightly browned.

4. Add garlic, onion, red pepper, bay leaves, paprika, and Cayenne to taste, and sauté another 5 minutes, or until onion is translucent.

5. Add tomatoes, reduce heat to medium-low, and simmer, stirring occasionally, 3 to 4 minutes, or until tomatoes begin to soften.

6. Add lemon juice, chopped parsley stems, pepper to taste, and ¾ cup dry red wine, and cook uncovered, stirring occasionally, about 5 minutes, or until liquid is reduced slightly.

7. Stir clams and mussels into sauce, cover tightly, and cook over medium-low heat until shells open and meat pulls away, about 10 minutes. Do not overcook, or shellfish will toughen.

8. Discard any clams or mussels that do not open. Adjust thickness and taste of sauce by adding remaining ¼ cup red wine, if desired. Sprinkle with chopped parsley and serve in casserole.

Saffron Rice

1 tablespoon olive oil
1 cup long-grain rice
½ teaspoon saffron threads, or ⅛ teaspoon powdered saffron
1¾ cups chicken stock

1. Heat olive oil in medium-size heavy-gauge casserole or saucepan over medium-high heat.

2. Add rice to pan and toast, stirring occasionally, until rice is opaque and slightly golden, about 5 minutes.

3. Stir in saffron and chicken stock, and cover pan. When mixture comes to a boil, reduce heat to low and simmer, covered, 15 to 20 minutes, or until all liquid is absorbed.

4. Remove pan from heat and set aside, covered, until ready to serve.

Wilted Spinach with Pine Nuts

2 pounds spinach, approximately
3 tablespoons virgin olive oil
2 to 3 tablespoons pine nuts
Grated zest of ½ lemon
1 tablespoon sherry vinegar or white wine vinegar
Pinch of salt
Freshly ground black pepper
Ground nutmeg

1. Soak spinach in sinkful of cold water and stir to loosen sand. Wash and trim spinach under running water, removing and discarding discolored leaves and coarse stems. Place spinach in large colander and set it in sink.

2. In large saucepan, bring 2 quarts water to a boil.

3. Pour half of boiling water over spinach. Shake colander to redistribute spinach and pour on remaining boiling water to wilt leaves. Shake colander to drain spinach.

4. Heat olive oil in medium-size heavy-gauge saucepan over medium heat. Stir in pine nuts and toast slowly, stirring occasionally, about 5 minutes, or until golden.

5. Add spinach, lemon zest, vinegar, salt, black pepper to taste, and nutmeg, and cook, stirring, just until heated through, 2 to 3 minutes.

ADDED TOUCH

Four anise-flavored ingredients give these individual flans, or custards, their distinctive taste. Anisette, a very sweet, colorless liqueur made from anise seeds and aromatic herbs, is sold in most liquor stores.

Creamy Anise Flans

Caramel:
½ cup sugar
1 teaspoon anisette liqueur
1 teaspoon whole anise seeds

Flan:
5 eggs
1 lemon
¼ cup plus 1 tablespoon sugar
¾ cup half-and-half or light cream
1 cup milk
2 tablespoons dry milk powder
¼ cup anisette liqueur
¼ teaspoon anise extract
Anise mint candies for garnish (optional)

1. Preheat oven to 325 degrees.

2. To make the caramel: Combine ½ cup sugar, 1 teaspoon anisette liqueur, anise seeds, and 1 tablespoon plus 1 teaspoon water in small saucepan. Bring mixture to a boil over high heat and cook, stirring constantly, 2 to 4 minutes, or just until golden.

3. Divide caramel among 4 large custard cups and set aside.

4. To make flans: Separate 2 eggs, placing yolks in medium-size bowl and reserving whites for another use. Squeeze enough lemon juice to measure 1 teaspoon. To the yolks, add 3 whole eggs, lemon juice, sugar, half-and-half, milk, milk powder, and anisette liqueur and anise extract, and whisk until blended. Carefully pour mixture over caramel into cups.

5. Line flameproof baking dish with folded tea towel. Set custard cups on towel and add enough hot water to reach halfway up sides of cups. Set dish on stovetop and bring water to a boil over medium-high heat. Reduce heat to low and simmer 8 minutes.

6. Place baking pan and contents in oven and bake until small knife inserted near edge of cup comes out clean, about 30 minutes.

7. Remove flans from oven and allow to cool in pan of water; the custard will continue to thicken as it cools.

8. When cooled, cover each cup and refrigerate overnight.

9. Serve flans cold in cups, or unmold and garnish with crushed anise mints, if desired.

Sausage-Stuffed Pork Rolls
Dutch Oven Cornbread
Mixed Green Salad Vinaigrette

For an early American touch, serve the stuffed pork rolls, cornbread, and tossed salad on rustic dinnerware.

In colonial days the sausage mixture would probably have been stuffed into casings or fried in patties, but here you wrap it in slices of pork.

WHAT TO DRINK

This hearty menu demands a robust wine: a California Zinfandel, Italian Dolcetto, or a good Côtes-du-Rhône.

SHOPPING LIST AND STAPLES

1 pound ground pork, not too lean
8 paper-thin slices boneless pork loin top loin roast, boneless pork shoulder, or leg of pork (¾ to 1 pound total weight)
Small head leaf lettuce, preferably red
Small bunch watercress
3 small bunches tart young greens, such as dandelion, sorrel, or arugula
Small bunch radishes with tops
Small bunch parsley
3 to 4 small cloves garlic
1 lemon
4 eggs
3 cups buttermilk
½ pint heavy cream
3 tablespoons unsalted butter or bacon drippings
3 tablespoons vegetable oil
3 tablespoons white wine vinegar
1 tablespoon mustard
1 cup white stone-ground cornmeal
2½ teaspoons sugar
1 teaspoon baking powder
½ teaspoon baking soda
1 tablespoon dried whole rosemary leaves
1 tablespoon dried whole sage
½ teaspoon dried whole thyme
¾ teaspoon freshly grated nutmeg
Salt and freshly ground black pepper
6 tablespoons dry red wine

UTENSILS

Food processor or blender
Large heavy-gauge skillet
Medium-size Dutch oven or cast-iron skillet
    with heavy cover
Small saucepan
Platter
3 large bowls
Medium-size bowl
2 small bowls
Salad spinner (optional)
Measuring cups and spoons
Chef's knife
Paring knife
2 wooden spoons
Metal tongs
Grater
Spice grinder or mortar and pestle

START-TO-FINISH STEPS

1. Follow cornbread recipe step 1.
2. Follow pork recipe steps 1 through 3.
3. Follow cornbread recipe steps 2 through 6.
4. While cornbread is baking, follow salad recipe steps 1 through 3.
5. Follow pork recipe step 4.
6. While pork is cooking, follow cornbread recipe step 7.
7. Follow salad recipe step 4, pork rolls recipe steps 5 through 7, and serve with cornbread.

RECIPES

Sausage-Stuffed Pork Rolls

½ teaspoon dried whole thyme
1 tablespoon dried whole rosemary leaves
1 tablespoon dried whole sage
¾ teaspoon freshly grated nutmeg
Salt and freshly ground black pepper
1 pound ground pork, not too lean
3 to 4 small cloves garlic, peeled and minced
½ cup minced parsley
Grated zest of 1 lemon
2 tablespoons freshly squeezed lemon juice
6 tablespoons dry red wine
8 paper-thin slices boneless pork loin top loin roast,
    boneless pork shoulder, or leg of pork (¾ to 1 pound
    total weight)
1 tablespoon vegetable oil

1. Blend seasonings in spice grinder or mortar.
2. In large bowl, combine ground pork, seasonings, garlic, ¼ cup parsley, lemon zest, 1 tablespoon lemon juice, and 3 tablespoons of dry red wine.
3. Divide sausage meat among pork slices and roll up against the grain. There is no need to tie or secure rolls.
4. Heat oil in large heavy-gauge skillet over medium-high

heat. Add pork rolls and brown evenly, 12 to 15 minutes. Pork is cooked when juices run clear.
5. Transfer pork to platter, cover with foil, and set aside.
6. Pour off all but 1 tablespoon of fat from skillet; add remaining red wine and lemon juice, and cook over high heat, stirring until liquid is reduced by half, 2 to 3 minutes. Stir in remaining parsley and cook another 2 minutes.
7. Divide pork rolls among dinner plates and top each serving with a spoonful of sauce.

Dutch Oven Cornbread

2 eggs
3 cups buttermilk
1 cup white stone-ground cornmeal
½ teaspoon salt
1 teaspoon baking powder
½ teaspoon baking soda
2 teaspoons sugar
3 tablespoons unsalted butter or bacon drippings,
    melted

1. Preheat oven to 425 degrees. Place medium-size Dutch oven or cast-iron skillet with cover in oven to heat.
2. In large bowl, beat eggs with whisk until foamy. Add buttermilk and beat to combine.
3. In medium-size bowl, mix dry ingredients.
4. Add dry ingredients to buttermilk mixture, and beat until smooth, about 1 minute.
5. Add half the butter to batter and stir to combine.
6. Add remaining butter to Dutch oven, pour in batter, cover, and bake until sides of cornbread are crusty and center has just set, about 15 minutes.
7. Uncover and continue baking until top is firm and inside is baked but still moist when tested with a wooden toothpick, 5 to 10 minutes.

Mixed Green Salad Vinaigrette

2 hard-boiled eggs
Small head leaf lettuce, washed and dried
Small bunch watercress, washed and dried
3 small bunches tart young greens, such as dandelions,
    sorrel, or arugula, washed, stemmed, and dried
Small bunch radishes with tops, washed and trimmed
2 hard-boiled eggs
1 tablespoon heavy cream
2 tablespoons vegetable oil
½ teaspoon sugar
1 tablespoon mustard
3 tablespoons white wine vinegar
Salt and freshly ground black pepper

1. Divide greens among 4 dinner plates and top with whole radishes.
2. Peel eggs, separate whites from yolks, and place in small bowls. Mash whites and yolks; set aside.
3. In food processor fitted with steel blade or in blender, blend mashed yolks with remaining ingredients.
4. Garnish greens with mashed egg whites and serve with the vinaigrette.

Acknowledgments

Special thanks to Alethea Sparks of the National Pork Producers Council, to Sara Lilygren of the American Meat Institute, and to Everett Lail of the USDA for their assistance in the preparation of this volume.

The Editors would also like to thank the following for their courtesy in lending items for photography: *Cover:* pan—Bon Marché; tiles—Country Floors. *Pages 18–19:* chopsticks—Five Eggs; napkin—Leacock & Co.; plates—Haviland & Co. *Page 22:* utensils, plates, mugs, pitcher—The Museum Store of the Museum of Modern Art; tablecloth—Conran's. *Page 24:* tablecloth—Conran's; platters—Rose Gong; teapot—Japan Interiors Gallery. *Pages 26–27:* plate—Mark Anderson; utensils—Wallace Silversmiths; napkins—Leacock & Co.; basket—Be Seated. *Page 30:* plates—Dan Bleier; glass—Gorham; paper—Four Hands Bindery; napkin—Ad Hoc Softwares; flatwear—Frank McIntosh at Henri Bendel. *Page 33:* platter—Dan Bleier; dishes—Harlequin, courtesy of Columbus Avenue General Store; tablecloth—Conran's. *Pages 36–37:* utensils—Gorham; plates, tablecloth—Conran's; napkins—Wolfman-Gold & Good Co. *Pages 40–41:* utensils—Gorham; napkins—

Leacock & Co. *Page 44:* black platters—Viking Glass, courtesy of Columbus Avenue General Store; utensils—Gorham; paper—Four Hands Bindery. *Pages 46–47:* linens—China Seas, Inc.; servers, bowl, board—Bowl & Board. *Page 50:* utensils—Gorham; dishes—Fritz & Floyd; glass—Conran's; tray—Pottery Barn; tablecloth—Brunschwig & Fils, Co.; napkin—Marimekko. *Page 53:* utensils, dishes, glass—Royal Copenhagen; obi—Japan Interiors Gallery. *Pages 56–57:* utensils, tray, plates, glass—Wolfman-Gold & Good Co. *Page 60:* platter, bowl, napkin—Pottery Barn; tablecloth—Conran's. *Page 63:* utensils—Gorham; placemat, napkin, plate—Ludwig Beck of Munich. *Pages 66–67:* flatwear—Ercuis; dishes, glass—Baccarat, Inc. *Page 70:* plates—Wedgwood; utensils—Gorham; napkin—Leacock & Co.; tabletop—Formica® Brand Laminate by Formica Corp.; glass—Conran's. *Page 72:* dishes—Haviland & Co.; utensils—Gorham; napkin—Pierre Deux. *Pages 74–75:* platters, linens, glasses, carafe—Pierre Deux; servers—The Lauffer Co. *Page 78:* plates, tablecloth—Conran's; utensils—The Lauffer Co. *Page 81:* platters, wooden bowl—Amigo Country, Brooklyn, N.Y.; mug, utensils—Conran's; peach napkin—Leacock & Co. *Pages 84–85:* glasses—

Conran's; tiles—Country Floors; platter, plates—Buffalo China. *Pages 88–89:* plates, bowl—Sointu; linens, utensils—Ludwig Beck of Munich; vase—The Museum Store of the Museum of Modern Art. *Page 91:* plates, glasses—Pottery Barn; utensils—Gorham; napkin—Broadway Panhandler; tiles—Country Floors. *Pages 94–95:* platters—Pfaltzgraff; plates, tablecloth—Columbus Avenue General Store; napkins—Pierre Deux; utensils—L.L. Bean; servers—Wallace Silversmiths. *Page 98:* white platter—Buffalo China; large black platter—Julien Mousa-Oghli, courtesy of Lee Bailey; small black platter—Ad Hoc Housewares. *Page 101:* plate, rug—Museum of American Folk Art Shop; utensils—Frank McIntosh at Henri Bendel. *Kitchen equipment courtesy of:* White-Westinghouse, Commercial Aluminum Cookware Co., Robot-Coupe, Caloric, Kitchen-Aid, J.A. Henckels Zwillingswerk, Inc., Schawbel Corp., Tappan, Rubbermaid, Litton Microwave Cooking, Farberware.

Illustrations by Ray Skibinski; photograph of Dennis Gilbert (page 5) by Chris Ayres. Production by Giga Communications

---

Mail-Order Sources for Country Ham and Other Cured Pork Products

Broadbent's B & B Food Products
Route 1
Cadiz, KY 42211
(502) 235-5294

Callaway Gardens Country Store
Pine Mountain, GA 31822
(800) 537-5353

Gwaltney of Smithfield, Ltd.
P.O. Box 489
Smithfield, VA 23430
(804) 357-3131

Joyner's Genuine Smithfield
R & R Limited
P.O. Box 752-C
Smithfield, VA 23430
(804) 357-5730

Smithfield Ham and Products Co., Inc.
P.O. Box 487
Smithfield, VA 23430
(804) 357-2121

Smithfield Packing Co., Inc.
P.O. Box 447
Smithfield, VA 23430
(804) 357-4321

Index

104

Time-Life Books Inc. offers a wide range of fine recordings, including a Big Band series. For subscription information, call 1-800-621-7026, or write TIME-LIFE MUSIC, Time & Life Building, Chicago, Illinois 60611.